History Hunter

History is all around you. The aim of this book is to help you to look for it and to find it. Of course a book cannot include everything, but it can help you to decide what to look for, so that you can make discoveries of your own. It is true that you can read a great deal about history in books, but it becomes very much more worthwhile and exciting if you go and see it for yourself. There is hardly anywhere in Britain that is not full of history, so that wherever you live your surroundings can tell you at least something about the past.

Houses, churches and chapels, railway stations, roads and street names, pillarboxes, fields and barns, ruined castles, fairs and market-places – all these, and so much more, can tell you something about people in the past and about the changes that have made the world you live in now. Here then is a guide to some of the day-to-day things – and some of the more unexpected ones – that you may discover.

Victor Neuburg is Senior Lecturer in the School of Librarianship, Polytechnic of North London.

House at Bocking, Essex, before and after restoration

Police station, Kentish Town, North London. The door on the right was for mounted police

History Hunter

Victor E. Neuburg

Illustrated by Trevor Ridley

for Alastair Mackenzie
from the author with
all good wishes
& hopes that he
will become an
historian. (13.1.79(.

Beaver Books

First published in 1979 by
The Hamlyn Publishing Group Limited
London · New York · Sydney · Toronto
Astronaut House, Feltham, Middlesex, England

© Copyright Text Victor E. Neuburg 1979
© Copyright Illustrations
The Hamlyn Publishing Group Limited 1979
ISBN 0 600 34557 2

Printed in England by
Cox & Wyman Limited,
London, Reading and Fakenham
Set in Monophoto Plantin Light
by Tradespools Limited, Frome, Somerset

For my granddaughters Katherine and Alison

Several people have helped with the making of this book,
and my thanks go to Stanley Brett, Sally Floyer, Roy
Gilbert and Adrian Mole. Barbara Gilbert watched over
the way it was written and typed the final version. My
wife Anne provided the support without which it could
not have been attempted.

Contents

Acknowledgements

The author and publishers are grateful to the following for permission to use material which is their copyright as reference for some of the drawings included in this book:

The Abbey Press for the map of the Ridge Way on page 54, modelled on a map in *The Prehistoric Ridge Way: A Journey* by Patrick Crampton (Abbey Press, 1962). Constable and Company Limited for the plan of the Battle of Naseby on page 111, modelled on a plan drawn by Patrick Leeson in *Guide to the Battlefields of Britain and Ireland* by Lt Col Howard Green (Constable, 1973).

J. M. Dent & Sons Limited for the plan of Saxon Winchester on page 38, modelled on a plan in *Alfred's Kingdom* by David A. Hinton (J. M. Dent & Sons Limited, 1977). Heinemann Educational Books Limited for the plans of the Tower of London and Durham Castle on page 107, modelled on maps in *The Castles of Great Britain* by Sidney Toy (Heinemann, 1953).

Her Majesty's Stationery Office for the map of Laxton on page 23, modelled on a map in *Laxton: A Guide* (HMSO, 1964).

Thomas Nelson & Sons Limited for maps of York (page 9) and London (page 10), modelled on maps in *The Geography Behind History* by W. G. East (Nelson, 1938). Thomas Sharp for maps of Heighington (page 31) and Coxwold (page 32), modelled on maps in *Anatomy of the Village* by Thomas Sharp (Penguin, 1946).

The warning notice on page 127 is reproduced by kind permission of Mr J. A. C. West, Curator of the Museum of Local History, Weymouth.

1 Settlements – why here and not there

One of the first questions a history hunter has to ask is why a town or village is situated in a particular place. Look at this picture of the pond at Ashmore, a village in Dorset. Ashmore was built at least 1600 years ago on a hill more than 200 metres above sea level. The earliest inhabitants needed a supply of water ready to hand, and the pond made living on the hilltop possible, and also provided a central point for the village.

Although it has been in existence for so long, Ashmore has never developed into a town. It is off the beaten track and far from any large town centre or industry or the sea. Other villages have grown into industrial towns, while some towns have shrunk into villages. This is because the balance between nature and

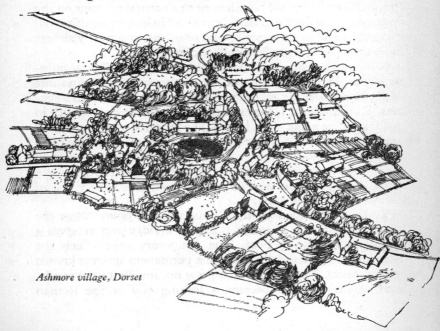

Ashmore village, Dorset

human activities changes all the time. Population grows, people earn their living in different ways, travel becomes quicker and simpler, and the landscape changes too. For example, a port may lose its importance because the sea moves away or because sand accumulates, making the passage of large ships impossible. Rye in Sussex was once a large port, but now it is some distance from the sea. At one time Chester was a major port for traffic to Ireland, but about five hundred years ago, a build-up of sand on the bed of the River Dee ended the city's days as a port. The building of railways in the nineteenth century could mean prosperity for some towns or death for others. Cerne Abbas in Dorset is a good example. It was an important glove-making town, but when the Great Western Railway was built it did not touch Cerne Abbas, which is still a very beautiful and sleepy little village.

There are many factors, then, which influence the site and the fortunes of a settlement. The founding of an abbey or the building of a castle; the establishment of a big market; nearness to a major road or road junction, or to a natural harbour on the coast or on a river; the availability of coal in large quantities – all these have affected the beginnings of towns, and nearly always more than one of these factors have played a part.

Sometimes towns have been deliberately founded by influential people, but they too would have thought first about some of the things already mentioned as necessary for a town's success. King Richard I, for example, landed near Portsmouth in 1189, and five years later, in 1194, he founded a town there by granting it a charter. The estuary on which it was situated was used for naval and military expeditions, and it certainly seemed likely that there would be people and activity enough for a town. King John issued a charter for a town called Liverpool on the Mersey river in 1207.

York was founded by the Romans at the point where the River Ouse breaks through a gap in a ridge and receives a tributary, the River Foss. The temporary base which the Romans set up here later became a permanent fortress known as Eboracum. The town which grew up, mainly to the south-west of the fortress, became a leading city of the Roman

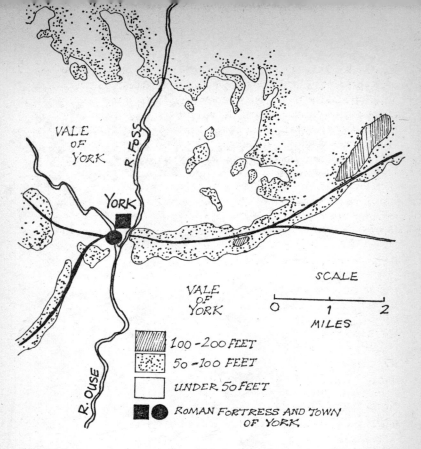

VALE OF YORK

R. FOSS

YORK

VALE OF YORK

SCALE

0   1   2

MILES

100-200 FEET

50-100 FEET

UNDER 50 FEET

ROMAN FORTRESS AND TOWN OF YORK

R. OUSE

Empire. As soon as it was established York became a route centre, and until the 1790s the only bridge across the Ouse was situated here.

Rivers have played a very big part in the siting of many towns in the British Isles. For example, Wallingford in Berkshire is on a natural ford across the River Thames, and because of this the town was built and grew. Sheffield lies at a point where small rivers or streams come together, but it was not their use as water transport so much as their provision of motive power for industry that helped to create the city. On the other hand, cities like Norwich and Canterbury are situated on firm, raised ground on or near rivers which could take small sea-going craft.

London was first built by the Romans on the River Thames. It was within reach of the south-east coast, but not so close that it could easily be attacked by invaders or raiding pirates. This map shows the geography behind the site of Roman London. The roads from the city follow the most suitable ground, and the early settlement was placed on the north bank of the river because building was easier here than it would have been on the marshy ground to the south. By the seventeenth century London

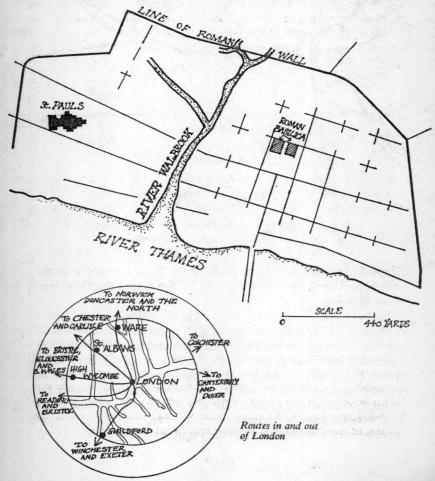

Routes in and out of London

was the focus for roads reaching out all over the country, many of which were very close to the roads built by the Romans.

A look at a map will often help you to see why a town or village should be situated where it is. Once activity of some kind has been established at a particular spot, the population is likely to increase. All those people will want somewhere to live, and so the settlement may grow; but, as I have mentioned earlier, places don't always keep on growing – they may decline instead. Look at these lists of the six biggest towns (excluding London) in England between 1377 and 1861, where the order is based on taxation and the size of the population:

1377	1523–27	1662	1801	1861
York	Norwich	Norwich	Manchester	Liverpool
Bristol	*Bristol*	York	Liverpool	Manchester
Coventry	Newcastle	*Bristol*	Birmingham	Birmingham
Norwich	Coventry	Newcastle	*Bristol*	Leeds
Lincoln	Exeter	Exeter	Leeds	Sheffield
Salisbury	Salisbury	Ipswich	Plymouth	*Bristol*

Only Bristol appears in all six lists, and by 1801 it is clearly the manufacturing towns of the North and the Midlands which have taken the lead. So you will see that there is nothing certain about the way places develop – there is a process of change going on all the time.

Cities like Manchester, Leeds or Birmingham were centres of the manufacturing industries from the end of the eighteenth century, and they attracted money and people so that their growth was spectacular. You might say that they were in the right place (near to raw materials and sources of power) at the right time (when technology was advancing rapidly).

The case of Margate in Kent is different. It is a seaside town which does not appear in any of the 'top town' lists, but its history has been a success story. In 1847 the first train bringing holiday-makers to Margate arrived, and this development in transport was obviously lucky for the town, but it had already been popular as a holiday resort for at least a hundred years.

Margate was, along with Scarborough and Brighton, the oldest of seaside resorts. From 1254 it had been a fishing village

('. . . one dirty narrow lane . . . was the principal part of the town,' as one account described it), but in the 1750s there was a craze for sea-bathing, which doctors said was especially good for health, and anyone who has spent a holiday there will know that Margate has sandy beaches. Here, then, was one reason for the popularity of the town, and another advantage was that Margate had by that time excellent communications with London, and was not too far from the capital. Besides the horse-drawn coach, there were the single-masted sailing ships known as hoys which carried corn to London and returned with goods for sale in the shops. These hoys also carried passengers who came to Margate for health and for pleasure. Fares were cheap, it was a convenient way to travel, and Margate prospered.

One of the pioneers of the tourist trade in Margate was a Mr Thomas Barker, a carpenter, who advertised in 1736:

> '. . . a very convenient bath, into which the sea water runs through a canal about 15 feet long. You descend into the bath from a private room adjoining to it. NB There are in the same house convenient lodgings to let.'

This was an alternative to open sea-bathing, and it was so successful that Mr Barker had to enlarge the bath the following year. By 1740 he was advertising 'good lodgings and entertainment at my house, which adjoins to the bath, and a good coach-house and stabling.'

So Margate's position on the coast, offering good sea-bathing combined with low-cost water travel to and from London, transformed it from a fishing village to a well-known holiday town; and when railways brought more visitors and day trippers the success story continued. Its own physical characteristics, together with the energy and determination of its residents, had made it a prosperous town.

However, no two stories of the how and why of human settlements are alike. If you want answers to the questions 'How did it happen?' and 'Why here?' look first of all at a map and see how the place you are interested in is related to other towns or villages, to roads, to railways, to rivers or to the sea. The map will give you some clues, and I hope this book gives you more.

2 Historic monuments

Among the historic monuments you can see in your history hunting are prehistoric burial sites, Roman remains, earthworks, Stonehenge and ruins of all kinds. Many of these are carefully preserved by the Department of the Environment, which publishes a useful leaflet called *List and map of historic monuments open to the public*. Costing only a few pence, it contains a very good folding map with details of what to see, where it is, and when it can be visited.

The best known of all historic monuments in this country is the stone circle at Stonehenge in Wiltshire. You may have been told that it was built by the Druids, but this is not so. It was erected, altered and rebuilt between about 1900 and 1400 B.C.

Stonehenge, Wiltshire

Think of it as a kind of cathedral which was in use for several centuries. Many of the stones are still standing today, and others lie where they have fallen. Spare a thought, too, for the technology which produced it. Think of the way in which the stones were transported to the site, some from Pembrokeshire and others from the area between Marlborough and Newbury. To have achieved this, by land and water, over long distances and without the help of machinery, is an amazing feat. Stonehenge is well worth visiting, and has a very special atmosphere.

Not very far from Stonehenge is Avebury. Here there is a huge earth bank and an inner ditch with four entrances enclosing a stone circle. The circle contains two more circles, and has a third at its north entrance. The whole site encompasses an area of over eleven hectares, and was probably built between 1700 and 1500 B.C., for what purpose we are not sure.

Avebury, Wiltshire

Silbury Hill, also in Wiltshire, is the greatest puzzle of all these monuments. There it stands, like a huge upside-down pudding, beside the Bath Road (A4), and nobody knows why it was put there. It is the biggest man-made mound in Europe: if you put Silbury Hill down in London's Trafalgar Square it would take up three-quarters of the space, and the top would reach as far as somewhere around three-quarters of the way to the top of Nelson's Column.

In 1968 and 1969 BBC Television organised an investigation of Silbury Hill. It was not the first – the hill had attracted the attention of curious people some three hundred years ago, but even with the help of modern science we know very little more about this mound than they did. One of the early investigators, William Stukeley, wrote in 1723 that the local people met on the top of the hill every Palm Sunday, 'when they make merry with

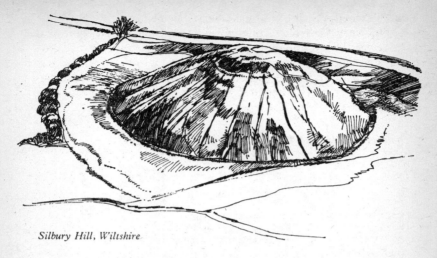

Silbury Hill, Wiltshire

cakes, figs, sugar and water fetched from the . . . spring of the Kennet.'

Prehistoric man has left other monuments behind him, and those you are most likely to come across are barrows and hill-forts.

Barrows are mounds, usually made of earth, which cover the remains of the dead. Some are 'long' and others round, according to the period in which they were built, and yet others were made of stone. The earliest barrows date from about 3000 B.C.,

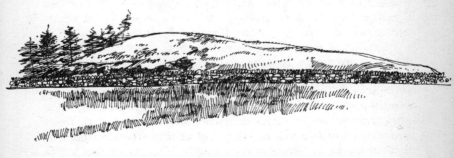

A long barrow

Inside a long barrow

and the men who built Stonehenge and Avebury would probably have been buried in long barrows. From about 2000 B.C. smaller round barrows were built, and although some of them have been damaged or destroyed by ploughing, lots of them can still be seen in the countryside throughout Britain.

Much larger than these burial mounds are the hillforts left by early man. These were not forts in which soldiers were stationed, but villages surrounded by ditches and banks which protected small groups of farmers and their families from attack by other tribes. Many of them also had wooden stockades as added protection, but in most cases these have disappeared. At Hollingbury Camp near Brighton in Sussex there are some remains of a protective fence, but it is the ditch and bank which give a clear idea of what these camps were like.

Near Letcombe Regis in Berkshire there is a good example of a hillfort. It is known as Letcombe Castle or Segsbury Camp, and running past it is the oldest prehistoric road in England – the Ridge Way. As you stand there, it is easy to picture the comings and goings of the families who once lived there. The site is now a field in which crops are growing, surrounded not by hedges, but by the earthworks dug as protection so long ago.

The most exciting of these forts is Maiden Castle, which stands on a hill near Dorchester in Dorset. It covers an area of about eighteen hectares and is surrounded by a ditch and ramparts. It was built over a long period of time, and was occupied by various tribes. In 42/43 A.D. its inhabitants were defeated by a Roman legion under Vespasian, and the survivors made their way down the hill to settle in the Roman town of Dorchester. In the museum there you can see some of the things which archaeologists have found on the site. Long after the battle, in about 367 A.D., a Roman temple was built at Maiden Castle.

The marvellous thing about this monument is the fact that it can be visited so easily and has never been built on, so that you can get a good idea of how it might have seemed to the tribesmen who lived there, and who one day watched the sun glittering on the armour of the Roman soldiers as they advanced to the attack. The remains of many of the defenders are buried in the war cemetery near the eastern entrance. Today, nearly two thousand years after the battle, the only sounds to be heard at Maiden Castle are the wind and the bleating of sheep. Even the car park used by visitors is at a distance so that no modern noise intrudes on the scene.

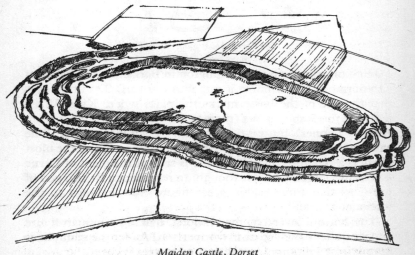

Maiden Castle, Dorset

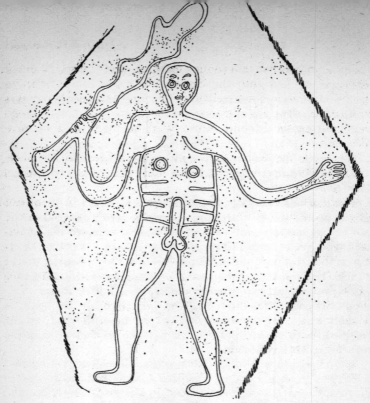

The Cerne Abbas giant, Dorset

High on another hill, at Uffington in Berkshire, the figure of an enormous white horse is cut into the turf. Tradition says that the site of the horse marks the place where King Alfred defeated the Danes in 871 (there was probably a white horse on Alfred's banner), but we do not know for sure if this is so. The early men who did it must have had a good reason, and the most likely is a religious one. The same is true of the giant of Cerne Abbas in Dorset, which is thought to represent a British god of pre-Christian times. This great figure now belongs to the National Trust.

The horse is over 100 metres long, making a human figure appear quite insignificant in comparison! As for the giant, he is approximately 55 metres tall and 51 metres wide.

The only other surviving giant is the Long Man of Wilmington. Cut into the Sussex chalk, he stands over 70 metres high and 35 metres wide. The figure you see today was restored in 1874 and survived being camouflaged with green paint during the Second World War, but its origins are prehistoric.

When you think about these sizes you will realise that planning the work and carrying it out must have required quite a bit of organisation.

There are other white horses in Britain, some of them not very old – several in Wiltshire, for instance, were carved in the nineteenth century. At Osmington, near Weymouth in Dorset, there is a white horse with George III on it, carved in 1815. It is the only white horse with a rider on it. Facing the sea, it was probably intended as an advertisement to ships coming into the harbour that the town was under royal patronage.

Another horse, carved at Lower Tysoe near Banbury in Warwickshire, was unique because it was coloured red. It disappeared long ago, but the surrounding area is still called the Vale of the Red Horse.

There are even a few twentieth-century hill figures which are worth looking out for. On the North Downs, about a kilometre south of Wye in Kent, the royal crown was made by students in 1902 to mark the coronation of Edward VII. It measures over 50 metres wide, and took six gangs of men four full working days to complete. During that time they moved four thousand barrow loads of earth!

At Dover in Kent, in Northfall Meadows below the northern side of the Castle, the figure of an aeroplane was cut in 1909 to celebrate the first cross-channel flight by a Frenchman, Louis Blériot.

During the First World War from 1914–1918, and just after, soldiers stationed on Salisbury Plain cut regimental badges and signs into the Wiltshire hillsides. The best collection of these is at Fovant Down, a smooth, steep hillside which runs parallel with the road from Salisbury to Shaftesbury. Altogether there are fourteen of these badges and signs, some of them carved by soldiers from Australia and New Zealand.

3 Farming

Nobody knows exactly when farming began. Some experts say about 12,000 years ago, but we cannot be sure, and it might have been even longer ago.

The earliest men and women were wanderers who roamed from place to place, gathering fruit and vegetables which grew wild. They were also hunters, and they fished in rivers and on the edges of the sea. Then there came a time when they realised that if they were to survive it was essential for them to produce more crops and plants for food. This brought about a revolutionary change in the history of man, because in order to cultivate the land, families had to stop their wandering life and stay put in one place. This led to the growth of settlements – small villages where the earliest farmers lived close by the fields in which they worked. First they had to sample and test what nature provided, and then they had to clear the ground, decide what to sow, prepare the soil and look after the crops until they ripened. These early people did their work so well that the men and women who have followed them, right up until today, have not added one single plant of importance to those which were cultivated by these prehistoric communities.

Archaeologists have discovered traces of early agriculture which tell us that the first farmers used tools to break the ground and sickles for reaping, and they also ground corn. They grew cereals – mostly wheat and barley – and left traces of their crops which can still be seen. The pattern of their fields shows up best when seen from the air like Saxon Down, Sussex, shown at the top of the opposite page. Outlines of the fields tilled by prehistoric farmers can also be seen in the early evening or morning when the light picks them out in shadow. They are most often to be found on chalk downs in the South of England.

There was another method of cultivation used by early people. They would make long terraces on the sides of hills

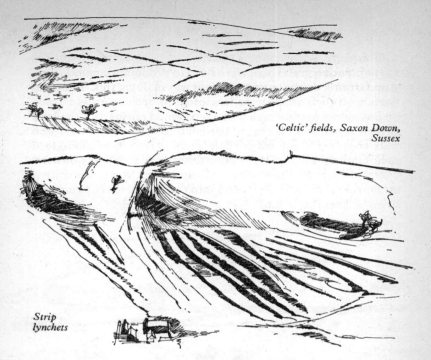

'Celtic' fields, Saxon Down, Sussex

Strip lynchets

where crops could be grown. These are called 'strip lynchets', and some of them have survived. In fact, they are much more easily spotted than the fields. These are near Chippenham in Wiltshire.

After the Roman occupation, the Anglo-Saxons came to Britain. They cleared forests and wooded valleys so that they could farm and grow crops. As the clearance went on, they built villages where several families could live in huts placed close together for protection. Their system was to cultivate big fields, but to divide each into strips, with each family owning one strip. So the land held by a family might be scattered over several fields, thus giving each the same chance to farm well, since nobody had the best fields! It also meant that the farmers had to co-operate pretty closely with each other, so that there could be agreement as to which crop should be grown where, and which fields should remain unsown, or fallow, for a year at a time to give the soil a 'breathing space'.

Gradually, however, this system came to an end, because as the population grew there was a need to produce more food, and strip farming was not a very efficient way of doing this. The open fields with their strips were 'enclosed' to become areas farmed by individual landowners who then rented out part of the land to their tenants. This caused hardship to peasant-farmers, who were concerned only with getting enough from the land to feed their families, but had at the same time to pay rent to the owners. Many of them had to work as labourers, and some just drifted away from the countryside and into towns where they earned a living as best they could.

Enclosure farming

Enclosure went on over several hundred years, and of course it changed the face of the countryside besides affecting people's lives. The landscape with fields that you see above was made by this process, and looks very different indeed from the landscape of open fields.

By chance, one open-field village was left, and is still farmed in the old way. It is now so much of a curiosity that experts come from all over the world to see it in action. This picture shows what Laxton in Nottinghamshire looks like. You can see

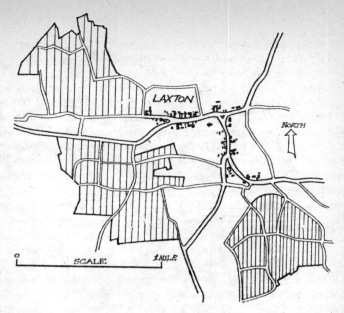

that there are three fields divided into strips, with the village in the centre. Today, a group of farmers, with the co-operation of a generous landlord, still make a living from a farming system which is obsolete. This is a way of life in which the cultivation of the land is closely bound up with the day-to-day concerns of the village. When you are sharing the farmed strips in the fields, you simply cannot go off and 'do your own thing'. Because Laxton is unique, it is well worth a visit.

19th-century farm, Nottinghamshire

Lower Tor Farm, Dartmoor

Quebec Farm, Leicestershire

The farms that you see today are all very different in building and layout. Page 23 shows an early nineteenth-century farm in Nottinghamshire. The farmhouse is on the right of the farm-yard, and the largest building is the barn, with its big door.

On the left are two very different farmhouses. Lower Tor Farm on Dartmoor was mentioned in a document dated 1249. The doorway was used by both men and animals – the animals turned left into their byre, and the living quarters for the farmer are on the right. This is one of the oldest farmhouses that you can expect to see.

Quebec Farm, in Selby, Leicestershire, was built in 1759. It is the kind of house that a rich eighteenth-century farmer would have lived in.

After the farmhouse, the barn is the most familiar of all farm buildings. Barns were originally used for storing and threshing corn, and this small one is at Cowdrey in Sussex. The thing to

A staddle barn

A cattle shelter

Stables

notice here is that the floor is raised from the ground and rests on staddle stones. This was done in order to keep the crop dry, and to prevent rats and other vermin from getting at it. The granary, where threshed grain was stored, was often built on staddle stones for the same reasons – you can see a rebuilt eighteenth-century granary in the Downland Museum at Singleton, Sussex.

Cows have always been important in British farming. They thrive on grass, which grows well in this country, and they produce milk, meat, leather and manure. Most of the old cattle sheds and shelters have been destroyed, or rebuilt to meet the demands of hygiene. This one (left) in the Cotswolds shows how simple the old buildings were compared with modern milking parlours. Occasionally cowsheds have been modernised.

Before trains made possible the rapid transport of milk to towns, cows were kept in cowhouses in towns so that milk could be sold over the counter, and it was not until 1953 that the last cow was milked in a cowhouse in the City of London. Even more recently the Express Dairy had a farm in Finchley, and it was possible to watch cows being milked, and then buy a glass of milk for a penny or two. The buildings, now empty, can still be seen near the North Circular Road.

Horses, too, have been important in farming, although for a very different purpose – the provision of power before tractors and harvesters arrived on the scene. Farming has now changed so much that few stables remain, but those opposite were built in Hampshire in 1838. In the area above, hay and straw were stored.

There are two other kinds of traditional building that you should look out for in agricultural areas. Dovecotes were first built nearly a thousand years ago. The pigeons they housed provided eggs, they could be eaten (and remember that before the days of refrigerators storage of food was a problem, and pigeons could be kept and killed as required for the table), and their manure was used on the farm. At first only the lord of the manor had dovecotes, but gradually they became a familiar sight on many farms. The dovecote shown overleaf, built in the sixteenth century, is more elegant than most.

Oast-houses were used for drying hops, which have been grown in this country for beer-making over the past four hundred years or so. The earliest oast-houses were built square, but these have all disappeared now and you will see – mostly in Kent – round ones dating from the 1790s. Because mechanical means of drying are now widely used, some of the oast-houses have been converted into picturesque country dwellings. The two below, near Goudhurst in Kent, fit in perfectly with their surroundings.

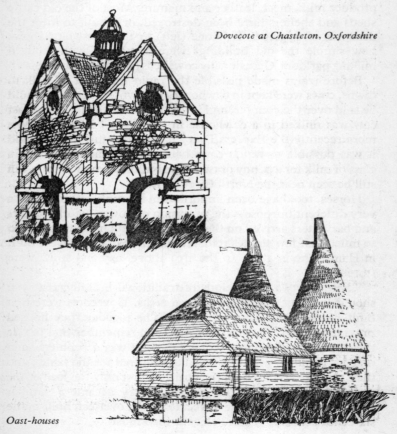

Dovecote at Chastleton, Oxfordshire

Oast-houses

4 Villages

Villages come in all shapes and sizes, but are usually smaller than towns and of two basic designs, to be described later.

Your mental picture of a typical village might be something like Blanchland in Northumberland, shown overleaf. Blanchland grew up at the gates of an abbey which was founded in 1165. The gateway which you can see in the centre of the village (arrowed) is all that is left now of the abbey buildings since their destruction more than four hundred years ago.

Some villages began as groups of peasant families who lived side by side, sharing and working the fields round about. The earliest surviving village in England is Chysauster, near Penzance in Cornwall, which was occupied from the first to the fourth centuries A.D. by farmers who also smelted tin. Today the site is looked after by the Department of the Environment, and is open to the public.

Other early villages have left traces only on the ground. At Bullock's Haste in the parish of Cottenham, Cambridgeshire (shown overleaf), you can see the outline of one dating from Roman times, and there are 'lost villages' like this in many parts of the country. But England is rich in villages which still look very much as they have done for a long time, and when you are looking at one, ask yourself first why the original settlers chose this particular spot.

If the village is built on light and easily-worked soil, then it may be that it has prehistoric origins – perhaps there are barrows or other monuments in the district which show the presence of early man. If, however, the soil is a heavy clay, in prehistoric times the site would have been waterlogged and heavily wooded, and it is unlikely that prehistoric man would have been able to cultivate it. The area is more likely to have been settled originally by the Saxons after the Romans had left Britain early in the fifth century.

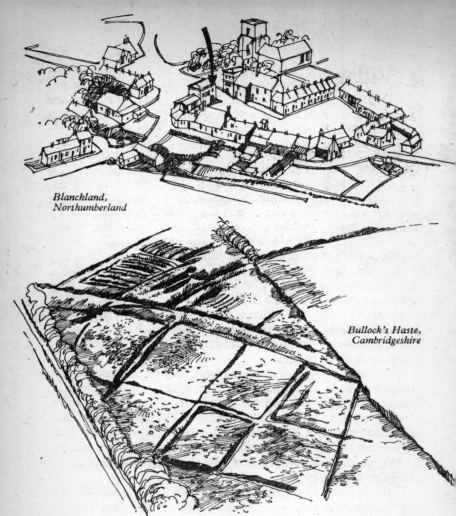

Blanchland,
Northumberland

Bullock's Haste,
Cambridgeshire

There would be many reasons why a particular site was selected for a village, such as climate, water supply, protection for flocks and herds, and nearness to road or tracks, markets (for selling produce) and the sea. When you are looking round a village keep the idea of these origins in mind, but don't be sidetracked by it. Think of what the village looks like today, walk round it and, best of all, draw a simple map of it.

Imagine that you have just visited Heighington in County Durham. Your map would look something like the one below. You can learn quite a lot from it. In the centre is the village green, and nearby the church, churchyard and school. This suggests that the green is older than the buildings. Next you will notice that Back Lane runs three-quarters of the way round the village, and marks the outer defence hedge or stockade which would have been necessary to protect the villagers and their animals from attacks by Scots from across the border. There is a pond on the green, so that water supplies would have been secure. This is a 'square' village – any arrangement of buildings on more than one side of an open space is known as a square village.

The other basic village pattern, which may be easier for you to draw, is the street village, where the buildings follow the line of the highway. Coxwold, in North Yorkshire, is a good example. Look at the map overleaf.

HEIGHINGTON
Co. Durham

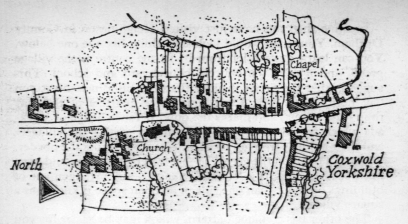

Chapel

North

Church

Coxwold Yorkshire

As in all villages, the church is in a prominent position, because for centuries it was the centre of social life. The chapel, a little way from the main street in Coxwold, was a much later addition.

What both villages have in common is compactness. This is because communities were smaller in the past, and people lived close together so that they could defend themselves more easily. For the same reason the fields where they worked were within sound and sight of home.

Once you have drawn a map of your village, go back and look again at any buildings or features which have interested you. The church and chapel are obvious examples, but have a look also at things like the width of roads. At Heighington, the roads leading to the village green are narrow, probably because they would have been easier to block in time of attack.

Another feature of every village is the inn. There may be more than one, but the most important is often near the church, so that worshippers could refresh themselves after a service – and, as you will remember, the church was at the centre of village life. Inn names can reflect farming activities, and you will find The Wheatsheaf, The Bull, Wagon and Horses, Barley Mow and Hop-Pole. National heroes or the battles by which they are best remembered, such as Nelson and Trafalgar, Wellington and Waterloo, are featured on inn signs; so too are Kings and Queens – but never Oliver Cromwell!

Two types of watermill: undershot (above) and overshot (below)

Essential to the life of the village was a mill, powered by wind or water. It would be situated on the outskirts of the village, and it was here that people would bring their corn to have it ground to make bread.

The water-mill is older than the windmill, and was brought to this country by the Romans. There are, as you can see, two kinds of water-mill, of which the second was very much more powerful because water could be collected behind a mill dam and then released onto the wheel from above. Not very many water-mills have survived. You may come across the remains of one, but often the only clue to its existence will be in a name like 'Mill Cottage' or 'Mill Lane'.

Milton Abbas in Dorset has a lovely 'old world' look, with thatched cottages side by side. It has an interesting story too. In 1333 it was a small town with four or five hundred inhabitants – a busy little place with a market, a fair and an abbey close by. By the end of the eighteenth century the abbey had become

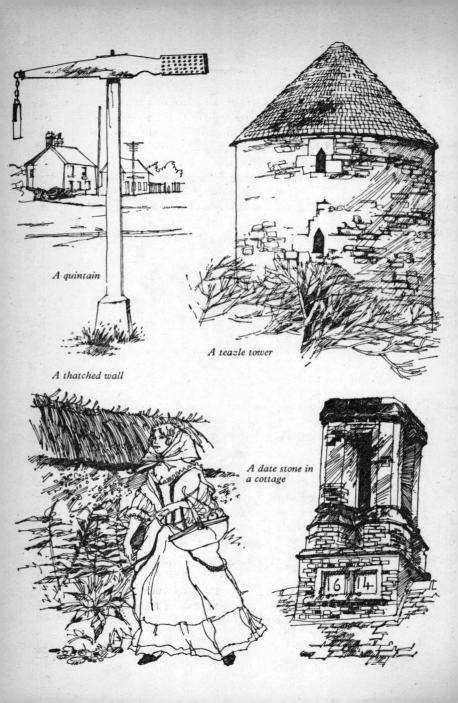

A quintain

A teazle tower

A thatched wall

A date stone in
a cottage

the home of the Earl of Dorchester, who disliked the noise and the bustle of the town outside his windows. So he had all the buildings destroyed, and built the model village that you can visit today about a kilometre away. The Earl's house has now become a school, and in its grounds it is still possible to trace the pattern of the original settlement in the banks, hollows and ditches which are easy to see as you walk around.

Sometimes when exploring a village you may find something unusual. At Offham in Kent is the only quintain still standing in its original position. A quintain consists of a post with a bar on top which turned on a pivot. A bag of sand was fitted to the end you see on the left, and on the other end was a flat board. In the Middle Ages a rider who took part in the sport known as tilting had to ride towards the quintain aiming a lance at the board, and pass on before the sandbag hit his head or his back. If he was hit, the blow was enough to knock him off his horse.

Another curious feature is the teazle tower at Woodchester in Gloucestershire. Teazles (or teasles) are the spiky heads of a plant grown mostly in the West of England. They were once used to brush the surface of newly woven woollen cloth to raise the 'nap'. Before use they had to be dried, and towers were built for this purpose. This is one of very few which remain.

In the south-west you might come across a thatched wall like the one in Netton, Wiltshire. Why thatch a wall? Simply because the building materials could be damaged by rain, and it was cheaper and easier to give the wall a 'roof' than to transport hardier building material from a distance – a very expensive and lengthy matter in the past.

You may find a house like the one in Steeple Bumpstead, Essex, with a very early date stone built into it. If the date, like this one, is between about 1570 and 1640, then it may indicate a new home built during a period of rising wealth for farmers.

Even if you are not going to find unusual features like these in every village, there is still much of interest to hunt for.

5 Towns and cities

People have been living in towns and cities for over two thousand years. In Britain our cities and towns are not nearly as old as, for example, Athens or Rome, for the very first were built by the Romans when they occupied this country for about four hundred years from 43 A.D. Today, apart from spectacular relics like the baths at Bath or the Newport Arch in Lincoln, Roman town buildings have disappeared, although where something like a piece of wall or a fragment of a house has survived, it is usually carefully preserved as a monument of some importance.

Newport Arch, Lincoln

The best guide to Roman foundation of a settlement is often its name. The Latin word 'castra' means camp, and it turns up in the names of towns and cities as 'chester', 'cester', 'caster' and 'caister'. Be careful, though! Blandford Forum in Dorset *sounds* Roman, but in fact it is not. York, too, could be misleading, for it was a very important centre in Roman times when it was called Eboracum, a name which remains today in the signature of its archbishop.

It is, however, still possible to see just how a Roman town was planned. Silchester in Hampshire – Calleva Atrebatum, as it was called in Roman times – was a busy town with more than thirty hectares of houses, shops, official buildings and public baths, surrounded by a wall with gates, from which five roads radiated like the spokes of a wheel. Silchester has long since disappeared, but because little has been built upon its site the pattern of streets can be traced without difficulty.

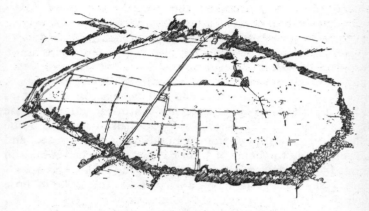

Plan of Silchester, Hampshire

This is about as near as we can get to a Roman town. Modern towns and cities are more complicated. They have been created over hundreds of years by a process of change, each period building upon the last, so that they have grown up layer upon layer. Buildings have been pulled down to make way for new ones, and although a few have survived, others have been so altered in appearance that it is not easy to tell how old a town is.

One good thing about recent changes has been that when buildings are demolished for redevelopment there may be the opportunity and the time to explore the foundations of older settlements. In this way the lost cities of Roman London, Saxon Winchester (see next page) and Viking York are being rediscovered by archaeologists.

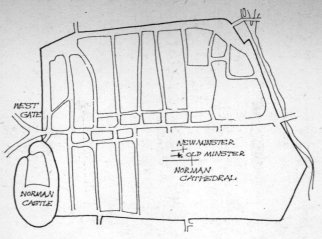

Plan of Saxon Winchester

It is unlikely, though, that you will come across any houses older than the fifteenth or sixteenth centuries, and even these are pretty unusual. This one at Coggeshall in Essex is a fine example. It is a timber-framed building, as you can see, and was originally the home of John Paycocke, who had it built in about 1500, and probably gave it to his son, Thomas, as a wedding present. Coggeshall, now a sleepy Essex town, was in those days an important centre of the cloth trade.

John Paycocke's house,
Coggeshall, Essex

Elm Hill, Norwich

Timber-framing was not intended to be ornamental: it was the skeleton which supported walls and floors, and could stand independently of them. The timbers were held together by mortices and pegging. Another example of such a house, built in about 1620, can be seen in Hereford. Now called 'The Old House', it is beautifully preserved as a museum and furnished with period furniture. The gables on the south side give a clear idea of the craftsmanship which went into the building of houses of this kind.

Buildings like these are well worth discovering, but it is also very helpful if you can find groups of them, where original roads or alleyways have been preserved, so that you have some idea of the landscape in which people used to live.

Elm Hill in Norwich, Norfolk, is a mixture of sixteenth, seventeenth and eighteenth century building styles, with cobbled streets and colour-washed buildings.

Picturesque landscapes and buildings are easy enough to spot. The real difficulty in discovering how old buildings are comes when you look at a more modern landscape which is likely to be a mixture of nineteenth- and twentieth-century buildings with an occasional survivor from the eighteenth! Many buildings from the last two centuries have been destroyed, but many more have been altered, so that we have to look for clues.

These two pictures will show you what can happen. You will see that the station building in Hackney, north London, has survived. So has most of the tall building on its right, but on the ground floor a modern shopfront has been put in, while to the

*Clapton station, Hackney,
in 1889 (above) and today*

right of this, the undertaker's premises have gone and there is now a much smaller watch-repairer's business. This gives us, incidentally, a much better view of the side of the tall building. Further again to the right, where there was waste land behind some hoardings, there is now a road. Finally, between the station and the tall building, where there was a space nearly one hundred years ago, there are now two small shops.

This is how towns and cities change, so that we are left with a mixture of old and new which, with practice, you will find exciting to sort out. If you are discovering an area which is a mixture of centuries and styles it is usually worthwhile to look above the shopfronts. As in this picture of Hackney, you may well find a building which is very much older than the smart shop windows which you notice first as you walk along the street. Holland Park in London, where eighteenth century houses can be seen above shopfronts and a petrol station, is another example.

Sometimes a building may be put to a different purpose, as the needs of the day change. In Saffron Walden, Essex, for example, a fine eighteenth-century house is now used as a post office, while at Bromley-by-Bow, in East London, a mill and oast-houses are now being used as offices.

Post Office, Saffron Walden, Essex

Some buildings survive by chance. In Preston, Lancashire, there is an old house near the city centre. Until a few years ago it was used for tradesmen's workshops, but today it is derelict. It was built in 1728 for the headmaster of the local school, and it was here in a back room, later in the same century, that Richard Arkwright built a spinning machine powered by water which made a fortune for him, and made mass production possible in the cloth factories. Today there are plans to restore the house as a museum to one of the great pioneers of industry.

Occasionally changes are dramatic. Hull, an ancient port, is an example. In the nineteenth century it was full of activity in the dock area, but today, because the docks are used much less, many buildings in the old town have disappeared. The pictures of Railway Dock and its warehouses show how much the landscape can change after demolition, and it is still not certain how much will eventually survive.

Richard Arkwright's house,
Preston, Lancashire, then and now

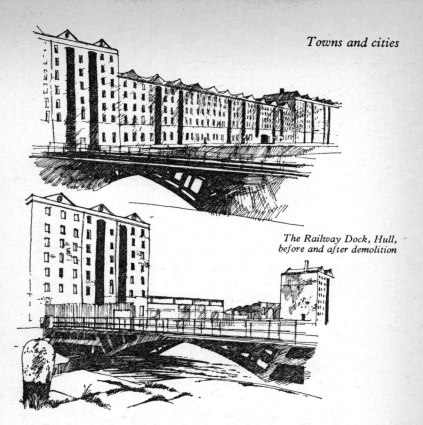

*The Railway Dock, Hull,
before and after demolition*

In this way, changes over the years have meant that our towns and cities have become a mixture, with old and new buildings often existing side by side. Over the page are two 'townscapes' of the kind you may come across.

The first one shows part of the Pepys Estate at Deptford in London. The terrace of old houses on the right was built in 1791, and has been incorporated into a development containing ten eight-storey blocks like the one on the left, and three twenty-four storey blocks, one of which can be seen in the background. These were built between 1969 and 1972. Elsewhere on the same estate is an old naval rum warehouse and a coach house which were built in about 1780, and have now been converted to provide flats, a library and a sailing centre.

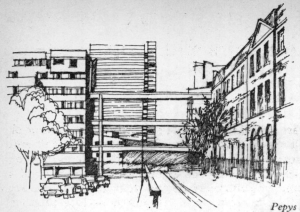

Pepys Estate, Deptford

In country towns there is always much to explore. Wotton-under-Edge in Gloucestershire is so old that the first town of that name was destroyed by fire in the reign of King John. During the thirteenth century a new town grew up, and today it has many fine old buildings and a wide variety of building styles. This view down Long Street and High Street gives some idea of the different patterns, and shows the countryside beyond.

See also: 6 Markets, fairs and shops
           8 Houses
        14 Street furniture

Wotton-under-Edge, Gloucestershire

6 Markets, fairs and shops

Markets

The chances are that if you go shopping with your mother or father you will visit a local market where meat, fish, fruit and vegetables, crockery, clothes and many other items can be bought from stalls. Whether the market is in the open or in a covered building, you should remember that some markets are very old indeed. Long before there were any shops, local produce was being bought and sold in markets.

Sometimes towns have grown up around markets. In Battle, Sussex, Duke William built an abbey to commemorate his victory over King Harold in 1066. Local people started to offer food for sale at the main gate, and before long a market had grown up and the earliest buildings of the town had been grouped round this market square. What you will see now is a square which serves as a car park by the gates of a ruined abbey.

This modern use of market places as car parks can be found in many other places today. For example, in towns such as Banbury, Hexham, King's Lynn and Northampton, markets are still held on certain days in the town centre, and at other times the area is available for car parking.

King's Lynn market

Some markets date from before 1086, but most of them were
founded between about 1200 and 1350. They were small, serving
just the local population, and there is no trace of most of them
today. However, the site of a market was often marked by a
cross – sometimes a simple column with a base for sellers to sit
on and show their wares, and sometimes a more elaborate piece
of stonework – and a few of these are still standing. The Bishop
of Chichester, Edward Story, gave his city a market cross over
five hundred years ago, and you can see it today in the city
centre, not far from the cathedral.

Another kind of early market is in Thaxted, Essex, underneath the old Guildhall. At Wotton-under-Edge in Gloucestershire the ground floor of the town hall was once open to the
street and served as a market. Covered markets like these

*Thaxted. The market was held
under the old Guildhall*

developed from the fifteenth century because people were
beginning to think more about comfort, and towns which could
afford it built some sort of shelter for the market folk. After all,
it must have been pretty miserable to stand about all day in the
rain and wind selling eggs or butter!

Fairs

The word 'fair' comes from a Latin one meaning holiday, and today the fair is a place where you go to have fun. People have done this ever since fairs began in Roman times, but in the past they had a serious side as well, for it was here that farmers and merchants did most of their business. Goods of all kinds were bought and sold, and drovers brought horses and cattle long distances. Horse fairs were specially important, because in the days before the motor car, horses provided the only means of transport.

A very wide main street like the one at Olney, Buckinghamshire, is usually a sign that a fair used to be held right in the centre of the town.

At the many fairs which are still held today we expect to find amusements such as roundabouts, swings, shooting galleries and so on, and we know that trade is carried on elsewhere. Only the names of some of the fairs remind us that they once had a more serious purpose. Horses were sold at the Horse Fair in Bampton, Oxfordshire, till 1957. There were no roundabouts or sideshows – just lines of horses with their buyers and sellers. Today a pleasure fair is held instead. The picture below shows St Giles' Fair in Oxford about twelve years ago, and this is still

St Giles Fair, Oxford

one of the most popular and best known fairs in England.

The great season for fairs is the autumn. This was the time, in days gone by, when the harvest had been gathered in and the farmers and traders needed to do business; but pleasure would be mixed with it and, of course, with winter coming on, this might be the last chance in the year to make merry. It was also the time when men and women changed their jobs, and it was the custom for farm labourers and others looking for work to attend the local hiring or 'mop' fair where employers would take them on. Each trade would wear a token so that its followers

Mop fair,
Marlborough

could be recognised. A shepherd, for example, would carry his crook and put a tuft of lambswool in his hat, a carter would have a piece of whipcord in his hat, and the cowman a tuft of cow hair. Maids carried a mop or wore a white apron, and at Wem in Shropshire this annual event was actually called the Rig or White Apron Fair. What is more, a name reminding us of these older customs is still used today in many towns. Mop Fairs are held at Banbury, Chipping Norton, Stratford-on-Avon, Marlborough, King's Norton and Worcester; and at Warwick the Mop Fair is followed a fortnight or so later by a Runaway Mop Fair. This second fair is a reminder of a custom which used to offer a second chance for those without work, or a chance to change jobs if either worker or employer was not satisfied.

The greatest fair in England used to be held at Sturbridge, two miles from Cambridge, in September. Traders came from as far away as Genoa, ports on the Baltic Sea, and from the Low Countries (now Belgium and Holland). Tin from Cornwall, lead from Derbyshire, salt from Worcestershire and a whole range of goods were bought and sold. In 1851 a man named Henry Gunning described it like this:

'As soon as you left Barnwell, there was a small public house on the right side, called the Racehorse; here the cheese fair began; from thence till you came opposite the road leading to Chesterton Ferry, the ground was exclusively occupied by dealers in that article. It was the great mart at which all dealers in cheese from Cottenham, Willingham, with other villages in the county and isle assembled; there were also traders from Leicestershire, Derbyshire, Cheshire and Gloucestershire. Not only did the inhabitants of the neighbouring counties supply themselves with their annual stock of cheese, but great quantities were sent up to London . . . In the neighbourhood of the Chapel, there were about a dozen booths called "Ironmongers Row": these, among a great variety of other articles, furnished the goods required by saddlers and harness makers . . . Another row of booths, reaching from the Chapel to Paper Mills Turnpike, was called "The

Duddery". These contained woollen cloths from Yorkshire and the Western Counties of England; but this part
of the fair was beginning to decline . . .'

Henry Gunning went on to describe the stalls where earthen-
ware and china from the Potteries were sold, the linendrapers,
silk-mercers, toy sellers, stationers and musical instrument
sellers. The largest booth belonged to a man called Green from
Limehouse in East London, who sold food and household
goods more cheaply than anyone else.

Sturbridge Fair had begun before 1211. By 1851, when
Henry Gunning wrote about it, it was losing its importance,
and four years later, in 1855, the fair was held for the last time.
All that is left of it today is the Common and a nearby Leper
Chapel.

Many fairs have survived, and although their function has
changed they are well worth visiting if you can manage it,
because they are links with a remote past and a tradition of
enjoyment. With the exception of January, there are fairs taking
place in England each month of the year; but for the reasons
already explained, most of them are crowded into the autumn
months of September and October. Some of the older fairs
which you could find are these: Bartholomew Fair at Newbury,
Berkshire, held early in September; Plum Harvest Fair at
Helston, Cornwall, held in July; Pleasure and Horse Fair (once
called Toro Fair) at Petersfield, Hampshire, held early in
October; Chanter Fair at St Ives, Huntingdon, held in
October; Pleasure and Pot Fair at Blackburn, Lancashire, held
on Easter Monday; Candlemas Fair at Stamford, Lincolnshire,
held in February; Goose Fair at Nottingham, held in October;
May Fair at Ludlow, Shropshire, held in April or May; Cheese
Fair at Yarm, Yorkshire, held in October.

There are, of course, many others; but remember that things
can change all the time, and if you want to be sure about a fair
that you want to visit, the best thing to do is to write to the Town
Clerk or the Parish Clerk of the place concerned (enclosing a
stamped addressed envelope), asking for details of time and
place to be sent to you.

Shops

Most of us go into shops at one time or another, and they are so familiar to us that we may take them for granted. People have been buying and selling and swapping things for thousands of years, so that the supermarket which we go into today to buy cornflakes, instant coffee, custard, bacon and jam has a very long tradition behind it.

Shops did not always look so glossy and colourful. Compare this grocer's shop with a supermarket of today. How many differences can you see? The older shop is darker; there are assistants waiting behind the counters to serve customers, and chairs for those who might have to wait; and the packaging is very different. When it opened in 1906 this grocer's shop was very modern, yet to us now it appears old-fashioned.

Sainsbury's, Guildford, in 1906

You may still find some old-fashioned shops, but they are becoming fewer and fewer, and even if the shopfront has not changed the inside has usually been modernised. However, even the exteriors will give you a good idea of what going shopping was like 100 or 200 years ago.

If you are lucky enough to visit the Castle Museum in York, you can see a number of old shops which have been saved from demolition or modernisation, and now form part of the museum.

Here are some shopfronts.

A

B

A An eighteenth-century bow-fronted shop with some fine carving (Stonegate, York). **B** Late eighteenth-century shops in Woburn, Bedfordshire. The market place was rebuilt after a fire in 1728. **C** Early Victorian shops (1857) in Butter Market, Reading. The fronts are made of cast iron. **D** A late Victorian shop (1891) in the High Street, Oxford. The shop-front looks very different today. Notice the door at the side of the shop in this picture: this would be the entrance used by the owner's family, who lived upstairs.

Look out for other examples of old shops. There are some still about, even though the scene is changing all the time and supermarket chains and department stores are taking their place.

C

D

7 Transport

Roads

This is a map of the Ridge Way, a prehistoric track which runs from Streatley in Berkshire sixty-five kilometres across the south of England to Avebury in Wiltshire. In the past it stretched from somewhere near Beachy Head in Sussex to Stonehenge and beyond, and it was used by men and women long before the Romans, with their skill in surveying and engineering, covered the country with a network of roads.

There were four main trackways like this one in Britain, as well as many smaller ones which have now disappeared or become part of our road system today. They were really natural

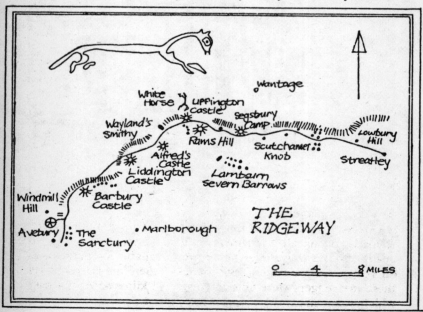

A stretch of Roman road at Blackstone Edge, near Rochdale, Lancashire

routes which could be followed without much difficulty because there was no need to chop down trees or bypass villages and no swamps or other obstructions in their way. The Ridge Way gives us an idea of how our distant ancestors travelled, and if you look at the map you will see that various prehistoric remains can be found along its route – a sign that this was once a busy road. Turn to page 57 for a bird's eye view of a Roman road.

The Romans were the first to *build* roads in this country, and they did this so that their armies could move easily and without fear of ambush from place to place. The roads were, of course, also used by travellers and merchants. You can see what a Roman road looked like in this picture of a stretch which has survived at Blackstone Edge, near Rochdale in Lancashire. It ran across the moors towards Ilkley in Yorkshire.

On the next page is a map of the chief roads built by the Romans. Along all of them at intervals there were inns and posting houses where fresh horses were available for messengers on government business. By changing their horses regularly these messengers were able to cover 150 kilometres in a day, which was then considered very fast indeed.

These roads were carefully planned and built, as you can see, layer upon layer so that the surface was higher than the land it went across. Because they were so solidly constructed they could not be washed away by bad weather, nor could the roadway itself, made up of heavy stone slabs, be turned into a swamp by heavy rains, as must have happened with ancient tracks. Most of the Roman road routes are still in use, with the stones laid by their soldiers and some of the local tribesmen now buried under modern roads.

Roman roads in Britain

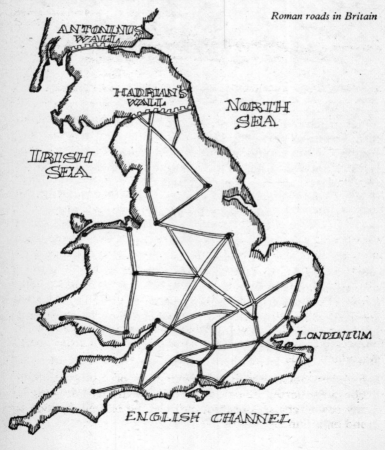

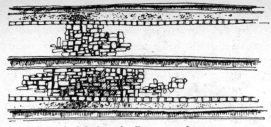

Aerial view of a Roman road

A section through a Roman road

After the Romans had gone nobody looked after this excellent road system, and for hundreds of years travel was expensive and uncomfortable. Those people who had to make journeys went on horseback if they could afford it, or if they were not so well off they walked or went in the carts and wagons which were used for the transport of goods. All of them had to face the danger of highwaymen and footpads lying in wait to rob travellers.

By 1663 the roads were in such a bad state everywhere that it was decided that those who used them should pay to keep them in repair. Barriers – called turnpikes – were placed across main roads, and everyone who wanted to pass through had to pay a toll. This of course required a collector to be always on hand to take the money, and so toll houses were built in which such collectors lived. Some lovely examples of these little houses are dotted about the countryside. Near Bishop's Cleeve in Gloucestershire on the A435 is a toll house with a rather faded sign which reads:

For every horse or mule not drawing, 2d; on a Sunday, 3d.
For every horse, mule or other beast of draught drawing any coach, chaise, phaeton, curricle, gig or waggon, 6d; and on a Sunday, 9d.

A toll house

Most of the toll houses you see are now used as private homes, but amongst the few where money is still collected is the one at Swinford Toll Bridge near Eynsham, Oxfordshire. Its notice board refers to the 'Locomotive Act of 1861', but the house itself was built in 1765. After midnight, all traffic passes over the bridge free!

It is worth remembering that toll roads are still common in the United States of America, and these are open for twenty-four hours a day, every day of the year. There are no toll houses – the collectors have kiosks and work on a shift system, and because there are several lanes of traffic it is necessary for several collectors to be on duty at all times. But one toll road that I used in the State of Delaware was automatic – you put the money into a big scoop, a recorded voice boomed 'Thank you', and away you went!

By 1829 there were so many toll houses in this country that you could not go for more than ten or twelve kilometres on a road without having to pass one. Sometimes the dust raised by vehicles was such a nuisance that pumps were erected at turnpikes so that the roads could be watered frequently. Such a pump is still to be seen on the old Bath Turnpike.

In fact, turnpikes and toll houses did not help the state of the roads at first because local people, who collected the money and were responsible for the roads running through their parish, did not have much idea of how to look after them. Fortunately three men, quite separately, did have ideas about road-building, and these began to be put into practice towards the end of the eighteenth century.

The pump on the Bath Turnpike

The first was John Metcalfe, often known as Blind Jack of Knaresborough. He had served in the army in Scotland in 1745, and when he came home, despite his blindness, he was able to prove that his earlier experience as a builder of roads could be of great value. He was asked to help with many turnpike roads, and the measuring wheel that he used can be seen in the Castle Museum in his home town of Knaresborough, in Yorkshire.

Blind Jack and his measuring wheel

Then there were Thomas Telford and John McAdam. They had different ideas about the building of roads, but both methods were being used by the end of the eighteenth century and the beginning of the nineteenth. The term 'McAdam roads' will suggest that he was the more successful of the two. Certainly McAdam's roads were cheaper to build and needed less expensive maintenance than those of his rival, so that by the beginning of the twentieth century most of the roads in this country had been rebuilt according to his ideas. He thought that drainage was all-important, and that if the road surface and its foundation could be kept dry by ensuring that these layers were higher than the surrounding ground, wear and tear would be reduced and there would be no call for constant repairs.

Because many modern roads are built on older ones, you should always look, when you see an excavation going on, at the various layers which have made up the road.

This is the age of motorways. Perhaps some history hunter in the future will look at them with interest, but I have the feeling that the older roads will always be more fascinating. They have had strong links with local people, and have passed through towns and villages which are part of our history. Motorways, on the other hand, are merely ways of travelling between two points at a high speed, and they really have no contact with the people or places through which they pass.

Signposts and milestones are worth looking at. Everyone knows the story of Dick Whittington who sat on a milestone on Highgate Hill and listened to the bells of London. This milestone is still there, only now the carved figure of Dick's cat has been added to it! You can see it over the page.

A law passed in 1697 ordered that direction posts on stones should be placed at 'cross highways'. This was not carried out everywhere, and in 1766 and 1773 signposts and milestones were again made compulsory – and this time the law was obeyed. It is true that the Romans had put up milestones on their roads, but on most of them only the name of the ruling emperor was carved. One is still standing beside the Stonegate, the Roman road which ran from Corbridge in Northumberland to Carlisle in Cumbria. There are quite a few more, but most of these are now in museums.

The older sort of signpost looked like the one shown in the centre picture overleaf. From Devon, it is a modern copy, built in a traditional way. Also shown is an odd signpost near Clun in Shropshire, erected in 1800 by a local landowner and standing about 2·5 metres high. It has four flat, iron arms with the names pierced so that each one looks like a stencil. To anyone who does not know the area it is rather puzzling. The arm that you cannot see in the picture says CLUN; the one pointing towards you says LUDLOW; but who would have thought that CLUNGUNFORD and BISHOP'S CASTLE were on the others?

At Bredon, Worcestershire, a few kilometres north-east of

Devonshire signpost

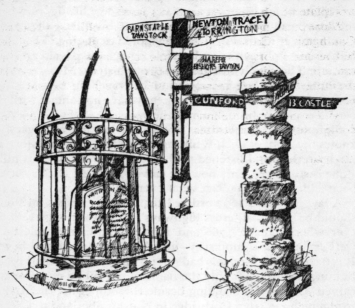

The Whittington stone.
Highgate

*Signpost in Clun,
Shropshire*

Tewkesbury on the B4080, is a most elegant milestone, complete with a date showing when it was put up.

'The White Lady of Esher' is really a rather grey milestone put up by the Duke of Newcastle near his private estate at Esher in the eighteenth century. It stands outside the Orleans Arms a little way north of the town. Nearly three metres high and one metre wide, it looks rather a self-important milestone, and although the date on the top reads 1767, it was in fact built some years earlier.

On the A22, about twenty kilometres north of Eastbourne in Sussex, is a good example of a 'puzzle' or 'rebus' milestone.

People who could not read might want to know the way. This one says 52 miles to London – the figure is plain enough, but London is represented by Bow Bells. The 'stone' is really a cast iron plate which was then fixed to a stone.

More puzzling is the sign at the side of an old coach road near Callington in Cornwall, just off the A390. Because of a steep hill, an extra horse was hitched to a coach or wagon to take it to the top. This sign marked the point where the horse could be unhitched and taken down the hill to await the arrival of the next vehicle.

Milestones are more interesting than you might think. They come in all shapes and sizes.

'The White Lady of Esher'

A 'puzzle' milestone

Rivers

More than seven hundred years ago Reach in Cambridgeshire
was an important river port. Today it is a rather sleepy village,
and the place where the quays and warehouses used to be is
shown in the picture. When roads were bad it was easier and
cheaper to send goods by river, and Reach is a reminder of those
far-off days.

Reach, Cambridgeshire

Crossing rivers has always been a problem. There were three
ways in which it could be done: you could wade across, take a
ferry or use a bridge. Nowadays we don't wade across rivers in
this country, but people did so in the past, and if they were
sensible they chose a 'ford', where it was known that the crossing was safe. Many town and village names end in 'ford', and
the chances are that the settlement grew up by a river crossing.
Think of names like Aberford, Cinderford, Old Ford, and so
on.

At Reedham, Norfolk, is one of the few remaining ferries.
Sometimes this word too crops up in place names. There is,
for example, Horseferry Road, which now leads to Lambeth
Bridge in London. There are Earlsferry and Queens Ferry – and
you will probably be able to think of others.

All over the country you will see bridges. Look at page 66. The oldest are similar to the packhorse bridge in Wasdale, Cumberland. On Dartmoor there are several clapper bridges, built wherever large slabs of stone were available.

One of the most beautiful bridges crosses the Great Ouse at St Ives, Huntingdonshire. It was built over five hundred years ago, in about 1415, and has a chapel halfway across it. There is another fine bridge at Wadebridge in Cornwall. This was built between 1468 and 1470, and was widened in 1847. The arches of the bridge are supported by stone pillars called piers, and on this Cornish bridge you can see that they are shaped like the bow of a ship. This was often done to divide the water as it rushed past, and helped to prevent the foundations from being washed away. Sometimes these cutwaters were carried on to the top of the bridge where, as you can see on page 66, they could provide refuge for a traveller on foot. If a galloping horse or laden cart came across a narrow bridge like this one, it would certainly be needed!

Vauxhall Bridge in London was opened in 1906. Notice the statues on its piers, the elaborate metal work of its arches and the huge stone cutwaters (page 66). Albert Bridge was built in 1873. Until 1879 it was a toll bridge, and you can still see the original toll houses at either end of it.

Bridges may not always be as spectacular as Tower Bridge in London, or the Swing Bridge across the River Tyne at Newcastle, but they are always interesting.

Canals

Canals are really artificial rivers which therefore have neither shallows to be avoided by heavily laden boats, nor currents. They were built as extensions to the rivers which carried so much traffic before roads and railways were fully developed. The first canal, which carried coal from the mines at Worsley into Manchester, about thirteen kilometres away, was opened in 1761. By 1789, as you can see from this map, there was a network of these man-made waterways.

An early canal was sometimes called a 'navigation', and the labourer who actually dug out the earth was called a 'navvy' – a

Packhorse bridge,
Cumberland

Clapper bridge, Dartmoor

Cutwaters

Vauxhall Bridge

word that we still use today. Men like the navvies who built the canals went on later to build the railways, which from 1830 to 1840 began to take over from the canals the job of transporting goods because they could offer a cheaper and faster service. Canals, of course, remained in use, but became less and less important.

Nevertheless, canals have left all kinds of marks on the countryside, and one of the best places to start looking for them is at Stoke Bruerne in Northamptonshire. Here, next to a lock on the Grand Union Canal, in an old grain warehouse and mill, the British Waterways Board has opened a museum. It is full of canal relics – prints, photographs, maps, documents, and all the colourful furnishings and decorations used by the canal folk

Canals in Britain, 1789

who made their homes on the narrow boats. You can also walk along the towpath and see the entrance to the tunnel, more than 3000 metres long, which is now the longest in use on the British Waterways system. One of the exhibits in the museum is a curved brush which was mounted on a boat and used to clean tunnels which had become covered in soot from steam craft.

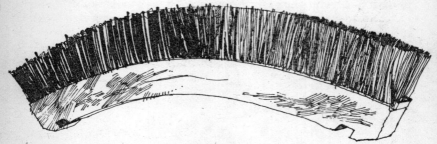

A canal brush

You will find canals all over the country, and when you explore, look particularly at locks, lock-keepers' cottages and warehouses. In Birmingham a derelict canal basin has been beautifully restored, and now gives a very good idea of what a busy canal port looked like in the past.

Only one English town was really created by canals. This is Stourport in Worcestershire, where the River Stour meets the River Severn. Before 1772 there was only a small ale house there, but in that year the Staffordshire and Worcestershire Canal was finished and a new town quickly grew up. It became the most important depot for goods in the West Midlands, connected by river and canal with most parts of the country.

There is another canal junction at Great Haywood, Staffordshire. Here the Trent and Mersey meets the Staffordshire and Worcestershire canal. Both canals were built under the direction of James Brindley (1716–1772), a self-taught engineer who was the first of the great canal builders.

Thomas Telford, who was mentioned earlier in connection with roads, was also keen on canals. In Wales, at Pontcysyllte,

A restored canal basin in Birmingham

his aqueduct carries the Llangollen Canal almost 37 metres above the River Dee.

This aqueduct and the junction of the two canals just mentioned will give you some idea of the canal landscapes you may find, but best of all you should walk along any canal tow-path, so that you can get the feel of what canals were really like

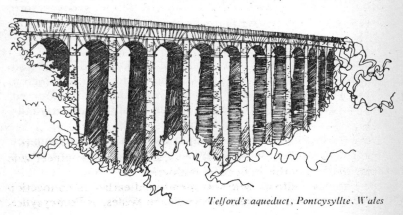

Telford's aqueduct, Pontcysyllte, Wales

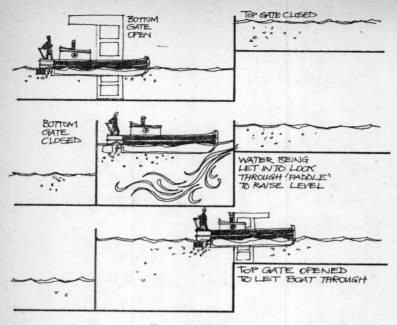

How a canal lock works

for the people who lived and worked on them. If you look carefully at bridges and tunnel entrances you will see grooves worn into the brickwork over many years of waterway traffic.

Railways

The first steam passenger railway, the Stockton and Darlington Railway, was opened in 1825. On the platform of Darlington Bank Top Station these two locomotives stand on rails mounted on stone blocks. They were built by the most famous early railway engineer, George Stephenson.

In the nearby town of Shildon in Durham are the remains of the Soho Works, founded by Timothy Hackworth, another pioneer of steam locomotives. His house still stands opposite the works, together with a row of single-storey workers' cottages with the original 'S. & D.R.' plaque on the wall.

The 'Agenoria 0–4–0', 1829

Because railways have changed so much over the years, many items no longer used have found their way to the Railway Museum at York. As well as twelve locomotives dating from 1822 to 1902 (see above and overleaf), you can see there many small reminders of railway history, such as name plates from stations which have been closed, buttons, lamps and prints, also early tracks, rolling stock and signalling equipment. You can even buy a souvenir ticket from a platform machine! The whole museum is housed in what used to be the workshops of the York and North Midland Railway, built in 1840.

Steam locomotives are now used only for trains run by

L.N.E.R. '2–2–2 Columbine', 1845

Severn Valley railway

Causey Arch, the
first railway bridge

enthusiasts who belong to railway preservation societies. Among these are the Bluebell (Sussex), Dart Valley (Devon), Severn Valley and Keighley and Worth Valley (Yorkshire). If you get the chance you should take a trip on one of these lines, and you will see just why it is that steam still attracts so many enthusiasts.

There is no end to railway history in Britain. Old Temple Meads Station in Bristol, opened in 1840, is the oldest surviving railway terminus in the world. Look at the bridge shown above – Causey Arch at Tanfield, County Durham. It was built in 1727, and years later railway lines were laid along its length, and so it became the first railway bridge in the world.

Last of all, there is the history of the London Underground Railway. The first part of it, called the Metropolitan, was built in 1863. From the start it was a huge success – on the day it opened 30,000 passengers used this steam-operated line running from Paddington Station via Edgware Road, Baker Street, Great Portland Street, King's Cross and Euston to Farringdon Street in the City. Since then the underground system has been electrified and has grown much bigger; but if you travel on the Metropolitan line, you can remember that this stretch is the oldest, even though there may be nothing in the buildings or equipment to tell you so.

See also: 11 Industry

73

8 Houses

There are two traditional ways of building a house, both of them very old. One is to make a framework of wood and then fill up the spaces with something flexible like wattle (interwoven twigs) or mud, or even bricks, which can be adapted easily to fit shapes of different sizes. This method is still in use today, except that steel or concrete is used for the frame, and the spaces are filled in with concrete, plate glass or some other modern material.

The other method is to build the house from a large number of small units such as bricks, blocks of stone or flints bonded together with mortar. In the days when transport over long distances was a problem, the material to be used depended upon what was available locally. Flint, for example, was widely used in south and east England, and if you visit the area of the Cotswolds you will find houses there built with stone which has its own local character.

There is a third modern method of construction: the various parts of the house – walls, floors, roof, window frames, doors – are made in factories, and the house is then put together on the building site. This way of building has the advantage of being quick, and 'prefabricated' houses were put up in large numbers after the Second World War, when there was a great housing shortage.

One day, more than two hundred years ago at Lullingstone Park in Kent, a workman putting up a fence came across part of a mosaic floor while he was digging. Nothing much was thought about it at the time, but in 1788 a man named John Thorpe mentioned it in a book. It was not until 1949, when the site was excavated, that the ruins of an entire Roman villa were found under the earth. The villa had been built in the first century A.D., lived in, altered and extended during the next three hundred years, and then deserted by its inhabitants after a fire at the beginning of the fifth century. Nobody knows whether the fire was accidental or whether the villa was deliberately burned down by invading tribesmen. At any rate, the site gradually became covered with earth, and was lost to history until its accidental discovery over one thousand years later.

We use the term 'villa' to describe a Roman house built in the country. The one at Lullingstone was pretty big, and the families who owned it through the years must have been important farmers. The picture below shows you what the villa may have looked like.

There are the remains of another fine Roman villa at Chedworth in Gloucestershire. This one was discovered in 1864 by a gamekeeper who, while digging for rabbits in an earth bank, uncovered some Roman paving. This time the owner of the land started excavating at once, and two years later the site of a large villa could be seen.

One of the interesting features of this villa is its central heating system. A paved floor was laid over these 'mushrooms' so that heat from a furnace fired by wood could circulate, warming the room above. Under-floor heating is still used today, powered by electricity rather than furnaces!

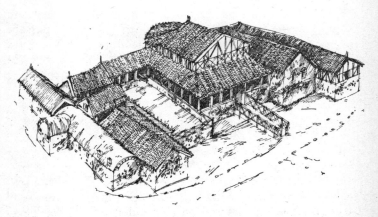

The Roman villa at Lullingstone

Roman underfloor central heating, Chedworth, Gloucestershire

After the Romans had left this country, their towns and buildings became ruins, either through neglect and the passage of time or because of destruction by invading tribes. We don't know much about the houses that these warlike people lived in after the departure of the Romans. Ordinary folk would have lived in huts which looked something like the one on page 77. This is a reconstruction based on two cottages which were excavated in the deserted village of Hangleton, Sussex – a site which is now part of the town of Hove, and is covered with modern houses and two golf courses. This kind of cottage would have been lived in more than 750 years ago, and it consisted of only one room. In one corner there is a baking oven, and in the middle of the floor an open hearth which was used for heating and cooking. Smoke escaped through triangular openings at each end of the roof. The doorway is very low –

145 cm – and there are two very small window spaces. These openings had to be small to keep in as much warmth as possible, and to keep out bad weather. Unfortunately, of course, light and fresh air were kept out as well!

This little hut helps us to understand several things. First, there is no chimney. Chimney pots were used on big houses about seven hundred years ago, but they did not come into use on small ones until centuries later.

Notice, too, that the roof is made of thatch. A thatched roof does not necessarily mean that a house is old. The Romans used roof tiles on their houses, and remember that the size of an ordinary tile measuring $10\frac{1}{2}''$ by $6\frac{1}{2}''$ by $\frac{1}{2}''$ (about $27 \times 16.5 \times 1$ cm) was standardised in 1477! However, thatch would have been used for roofing because material for it was ready to hand and conveniently cheap. It insulated the house beautifully, but had two main drawbacks which still apply today: there was always the danger of fire, and birds could damage it severely.

There is no glass in this cottage. Glazed windows did not become common until the end of the sixteenth century in large houses, and about a hundred years later in small ones.

Sash windows – those which slide up and down in a frame – first came into use at the end of the seventeenth century. The

Reconstruction of a 13-century cottage

large panes of glass that you see in many windows today were not available until 1840.

In 1840 windows were still being taxed. The Window Tax was first imposed in 1695 to cover the cost of replacing coins which people had deliberately damaged. (It seems they clipped the edges off the coins and collected the fragments of gold and silver for melting down.) The Window Tax was felt to be so successful that by 1808 it had been increased six times. In 1823 it was reduced, and it was finally abolished in 1851. Because this tax was levied on the number of windows in houses, some were designed with fewer windows than they might otherwise have had, while in houses already in existence, some of the windows were bricked up to avoid paying tax.

Windows are a useful guide to the history of a house, but of course you will come across old houses which have had modern windows put into them, for large windows provide light and fresh air. On the other hand, sometimes you will see a twentieth-century house like the one shown at the bottom of page 80 which has been built with old-fashioned windows!

Houses are always being altered for one reason or another. Modernisation of old ones makes life very much more comfortable for those who live in them, but it makes things more difficult for the history hunter. For example, in Thaxted,

A 14th-century, B 15th-century, C 16th-century,
D 17th-century, E late 17th-century, early 18th-century,
F 18th-century, G late 18th-century, early 19th-century,
H 19th-century plate glass

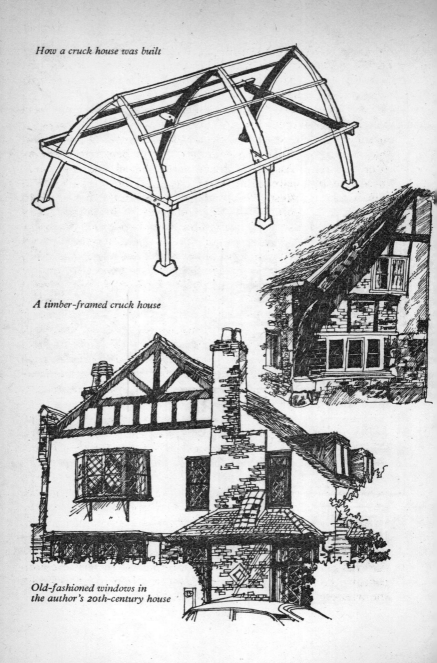

How a cruck house was built

A timber-framed cruck house

**Old-fashioned windows in
the author's 20th-century house**

Essex, is a lovely example of a small eighteenth-century building, but in 1938 it was discovered that the inside had features which dated from 1480. This shows us that we can never be too exact about the age of houses.

Even the material from which a house is built does not always help. Brick has been used for centuries, and you should remember that the size of bricks was standardised in 1637, and that the use of small, sub-standard bricks began to decrease after this date. Also, as we saw earlier, local materials were then used in construction. Flint was common in Sussex, and this house in West Dean village, built in the seventeenth century, has a mixture of flint and brick in its fabric. Early brickwork can always be spotted quite easily because the bricks were irregular in size, colour and texture, and they were thinner than the standard ones; but, as you saw in Chapter 5, it is not likely that you will come across many houses more than four or five hundred years old, and few of these are in their original condition. Look again at John Paycocke's timber-framed house on page 38 and then look at the one shown in the middle of page 80. It is a timber-framed cruck building. The cruck was a curved oak trunk split down the middle, the two halves put up to meet at the top. The picture at the top of the opposite page shows how cruck houses were built. The spaces between the timbers were then filled in with cross beams, as mentioned at the beginning of this chapter.

Timber-framed buildings with or without crucks show old techniques which have been in use for over five hundred years. On page 82(C) is a farmhouse which has been rebuilt at the Downland Museum at Singleton in Sussex. It was first built between 1420 and 1480, and much altered two hundred years later. On the left, jutting out, is an old lavatory called a garderobe. This is the kind of house that a prosperous farmer in the reign of Queen Elizabeth I lived in.

Pages 82–3 show some other houses which will help you to decide about the age of buildings you may see.

A This house was built in the middle of the seventeenth century. It has a very imposing front, but you will notice that the windows have been altered since 1840.

A Mid 17th-century house,
B Mid 18th-century house,
C 15th-century house, D 1830s houses,
E 19th-century terraces, F Victorian semi

B This house was built in 1753, and like so many eighteenth-century houses it is beautifully proportioned.

C Fifteenth-century with seventeenth-century alterations.

D Part of a square of houses built for the prosperous middle classes to live in during the 1830s.

E A contrast! Terraced cottages built for workers in nineteenth-century York.

F A Victorian semi-detached house.

Semi-detached houses became more and more common from the nineteenth century onwards when the population, particularly in towns and cities, was steadily increasing, for they were cheaper to build than detached ones and better use could be made of building land which was becoming scarcer and more expensive. Their occupants could at least enjoy more privacy than they would have had in the long terraces of houses which were also common at that time and which have now for the most part been swept away by slum clearance schemes.

Don't forget that blocks of flats built in the nineteenth century are still used, although the insides are usually very much altered for comfort, and bathrooms have been added.

Throughout history people have needed homes to provide shelter, warmth and privacy, and in this chapter we have been looking at some of the different kinds of houses which have helped to satisfy these needs.

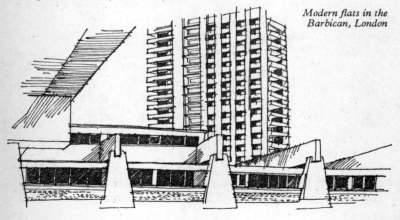

Modern flats in the Barbican, London

9 Religion

The pagan past

We don't know much about the pagan religions which were widely practised in this country before Christianity was established, but relics of them can still be seen. Stonehenge, Avebury and Silbury Hill have all been mentioned in Chapter 2, and you can see several other reminders of these vanished religions.

For example, in the twelfth-century church at Kilpeck, Herefordshire, is a small statue of a god which looks as though it has no business in a church! Other pagan relics you might see are puzzling rock carvings like the ones on the island of Eday, Orkney, or the Maiden Stone near Inverurie, Aberdeenshire. In Newcastle upon Tyne, off the West Road, are the remains of a Roman temple. In the City of London, remains of a temple dedicated to a god named Mithras, worshipped by Roman soldiers, were discovered in 1954 during rebuilding. Today you can visit these remains on the south side of Queen Victoria Street. Look at the pictures overleaf.

Finding relics from a pagan past is always exciting. You will not, of course, find many, for apart from their natural disappearance with the passing of time, some of them were destroyed by early Christians who wanted to establish their religion as the only true one in these islands.

Christian churches

Christianity was known in Britain during the Roman occupation. Three bishops from this country – all of whom, it is said, were too poor to pay their own travelling expenses – attended a meeting of Christians in France in 314; and remains of a chapel have been discovered on the site of a wealthy fourth-century Roman villa at Lullingstone in Kent. After the Romans left things went badly and the country was invaded.

The Maiden Stone near Inverurie,
Aberdeenshire

Statue in 12th-century church,
Kilpeck, Herefordshire

Roman temple,
Newcastle upon Tyne

The Christian church suffered during these disturbed times, and in 596 Saint Augustine landed in the Isle of Thanet in order to restore the faith. About three kilometres from Ebbsfleet on the Ramsgate-to-Sandwich Road is St Augustine's Cross, which was erected in 1884 to mark the spot where the saint met King Ethelbert and preached his first sermon.

This country now has a wealth of churches to show just how effective Saint Augustine's mission was. Very few of the early Saxon churches are left, as many were built of wood, which could hardly survive over so many centuries; and others built

Saxon church, Greensted, Essex

of stone have been altered out of all recognition. Only one timber church is left, and this is St Andrew at Greensted-Juxta-Ongar in Essex. The walls you see in this picture are made of split logs. Another Saxon church, this time built of stone taken partly from the nearby Roman fort at Binchester, can be found in a tiny village called Escombe, in Durham. It is a very bare and simple building which, except for the windows which were put in at a later date, has stayed pretty well untouched since Saxon times. And this is how an unknown artist of the time saw part of the congregation in a church like that at Escombe.

An early congregation carved in stone, Northumbria

Holy Sepulchre Church in Cambridge is unusual because it is round. Only four churches shaped like this are still in use in England, the other three being in Northampton, in Little Maplestead, Essex, and the Temple Church in London. The Cambridge church is over eight hundred years old, and certainly looks different from the churches you will find in your own neighbourhood, for although these vary in age and appearance they follow a basic pattern.

Holy Sepulchre church, Cambridge

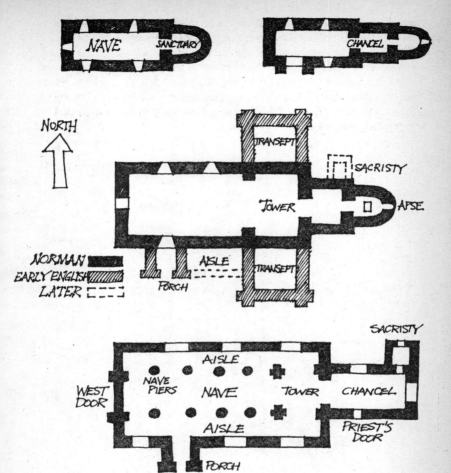

The growth of the parish church

Besides growing outwards, churches sometimes grew upwards. From about 1430 a clerestory might be added – an extension to the wall of the nave, pierced by windows, so that the church was higher and also able to receive more daylight.

A

B

C

D

E

F

G

H

Buttresses and columns.
A Simple Norman, B & E Early English,
C Decorated, D & G Perpendicular,
F Norman, H Anglo-Saxon

Other clues to the age of a church are windows and doors. As you can see from this picture, the Norman style is distinctive. Other styles in church building followed the Norman period, and 'Early English' indicates thirteenth century, while 'Perpendicular' is a design which came into fashion between 1350 and 1530. But remember that, just because a window or a door looks Early English or Perpendicular, it is not necessarily original. It might be a copy of one of these styles built at a later time, and the easiest way to make sure is to consult a guide to its history (usually costing only a few pence), which you will find in most

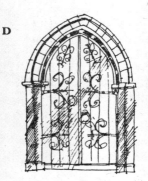 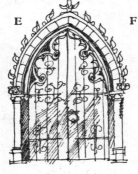 

Windows and doors:
A Norman, B & D Early English, C & F Perpendicular, E Decorated

churches, so that you can see when the building originated and how it has developed since then.

Such a guide will also mention the interesting features of the church, like the Anglo-Saxon crypt at Repton, Derbyshire, or the very old pews and benches in the fifteenth-century church at Badley in Suffolk, shown opposite.

Inside the church, look out for carvings, ironwork, old notices, and any unusual features such as the church chest at Greystoke, Cumberland. Some of these chests are marvellous pieces of work, bound with iron and provided with three or more padlocks, each with a different key. The keys were given to different people so that all had to be present when the chest was opened. At Warbleton in Sussex the chest has seven padlocks! Clearly the safety which such chests provided was regarded as important, and in 1287 it was ordered that one should be placed in each church for the safekeeping of robes, books and any valuable plate which the church owned.

Amongst some of the less obvious things that you can find in a church are memorial tablets to people of all kinds. Chigwell is about eleven kilometres to the north-east of London, and has a fifteenth-century church. Inside is a tablet erected by London busmen to commemorate George Shillibeer, who started the first omnibus service in London in 1829. Each of his buses could take twenty-two passengers and was drawn by three horses. They covered the route from the Bank of England to Paddington. The fare was five pence, and when Shillibeer began the service the only competition was stagecoaches which charged twelve and a half pence for the same journey.

In old churches you will sometimes come across 'graffiti' – words or pictures scratched on the walls. At Ashwell, Hertfordshire, there is a picture of the spire of the old St Paul's which was destroyed in the Fire of London.

Outside churches you are visiting, look at the clock in the tower. Even if it is a new one, it is part of a long tradition. It has always been important to let people know the time so that they could attend services without being late, and originally this was done with a sundial. You may find traces of an old sundial in the wall, sometimes almost worn away by wind and weather. The

15th-century church, Badley, Suffolk

Church chest, Greystoke, Cumberland

A sundial

*Graffito of old
St Paul's with
its spire*

more modern one pictured at the bottom of page 93 shows exactly how they worked.

Clocks date from the twelfth century, but at that time they had no dials and used to mark the passing of the hours by striking a bell. One such clock, built before 1386, is still in working order in Salisbury Cathedral. Early clocks with dials had only one hand, like the one at Coningsby, Lincolnshire. Really accurate timekeeping dates from 1657, when a new mechanism was invented. The first clock with two dials which measured both hours and minutes was put up outside the church of St Dunstan-in-the-West, Fleet Street, London, where you can see it now, still telling the time.

There are some oddities amongst clocks. A clock at Whixley in Yorkshire has a message under the dial, but the strangest ones of all are those which have letters instead of figures on the dial, spelling out a message. There is one at Baslow in Derbyshire which was made to celebrate the sixtieth year of Queen Victoria's reign: instead of numerals round the clock face you can read 'Victoria 1897'. At Wooton Rivers in Wiltshire, there is a church clock built from scrap material in 1911 by a local man named Jack Spratt. The pendulum is made of a broom handle, and one of the faces on the clock reads 'Glory be to God'. Clocks can be fascinating. Look at them carefully.

In the churchyard you might come across a wooden grave-board (see opposite). It would have been put up by people who could not afford a stone memorial, and the painted inscription can hardly be made out because it has worn away. Even tomb-stones with carving sometimes weather badly, but those which can be read tell us something about the men, women and children who lived their lives in the parish and were eventually buried in the grounds of their church.

At the entrance to the churchyard you will often find a lych-gate which dates from the seventeenth or eighteenth century. The story of lych-gates is rather gruesome. 'Lych' is Anglo-Saxon for corpse, and when a funeral took place, coffin-bearers and mourners would wait at these gates until the priest was ready for them. Since nobody liked hanging about in bad weather, a shelter was provided. Lych-gates often look rather picturesque.

Clock, Coningsby, Lincolnshire

Jack Spratt's clock

Wooden graveboard

Lych-gate,
Ightham, Kent

A lych-gate at Holy Trinity Church, Clifton, Derbyshire, has a clock which was installed in 1924, although the gate itself is much older. At Atherington in North Devon the table where the corpse was put while the burial party waited can still be seen under the gate.

Cathedrals

Cathedrals are so rich in history that when you visit one it is easy to waste time by not knowing quite what to look for. To avoid this, do buy a guide from the cathedral bookstall. In most cases – at York Minster, for example – you will find a booklet specially written for young people, which is helpful and not expensive.

A general rule when looking round a cathedral is to stand first of all in the nave near the central tower, and try to get some idea of the 'feel' of the place. You will see different styles of architecture and different ways of building. Notice the altar, the stained glass windows, the pillars which support the roof, and of course the roof itself. By then you will begin to know the groundplan of the cathedral, and can start to walk round looking for some of the treasures you will surely find.

There will be tombs and monuments, and you may also see the 'colours' or flags of local regiments, which were carried at battles like Waterloo, and are now quite often threadbare. At Westminster Abbey there is Poets' Corner. There is no shortage of things to see, but you will need the help of a guide if you are to make sense of so much.

Don't overlook the Chapter House. The Dean and a group of colleagues are called the Chapter, and their task is to look after the cathedral and its work. The Chapter House at Salisbury is particularly worth seeing, and at Hereford there is a library of books which are chained to the shelves so that they cannot be removed. This is a reminder of the time when books were rare and needed to be kept secure. The library at Hereford is more than four hundred years old and contains over 1440 books. Survivals like this make cathedrals exciting places to visit, for you can see and sense a history which has extended over hundreds of years, and still lives on.

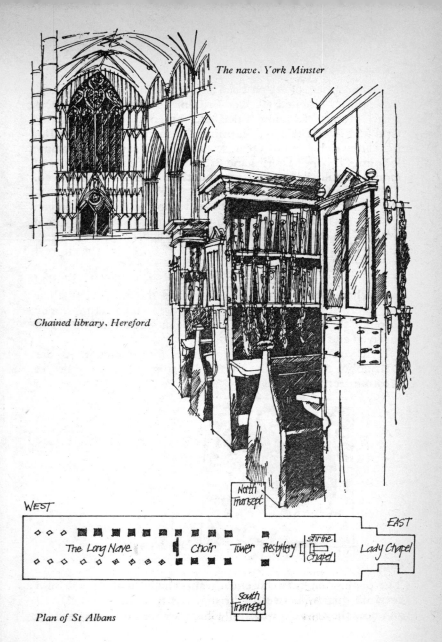

The nave, York Minster

Chained library, Hereford

WEST

North
Transept

EAST

The Long Nave   Choir   Tower   Presbytery   Shrine Chapel   Lady Chapel

South
Transept

Plan of St Albans

97

Ruins of Christianity

The atmosphere of the past can also be felt in the ruined abbeys and priories situated all over Britain. They were once places where groups of monks, ruled over by an abbot, worshipped God and lived their lives farming the surrounding lands. But they grew rich and powerful, so that King Henry VIII became jealous of the monasteries and ordered that the communities of monks should be broken up and their buildings destroyed. Today if you visit the ruins of an abbey or a monastery, remember that the piles of stone, ruined towers and jagged walls were the home of generations of monks, the last of whom were driven out over four hundred years ago.

The ruins of Fountains Abbey in Yorkshire give the clearest idea of how the monks lived. It was here a few years ago that a strain of bees was discovered which experts believed had died out. When the abbey was destroyed and the monks left, their bees were somehow overlooked, and went on making honey through the centuries until someone noticed that they had survived and were still busy.

Here you can see an early picture of monks meeting under their abbot to discuss the day-to-day running of the abbey at Westminster.

Monks with their Abbot

Chapels

The distinction between church and chapel is the result of a very old quarrel between Christians as to what they believed and how they should worship. Chapels were built and used by

Baptist chapel, Tewkesbury, Gloucestershire

'nonconformists', who saw themselves as breaking away from the Church of England. The more important groups of non-conformists called themselves Congregationalists, Baptists, Unitarians, Methodists, Presbyterians, and so on.

Nonconformist chapels – a few of which date from the seventeenth century – are very different in appearance from churches, and just as worthwhile to look at. They come in different shapes and sizes, and are generally much simpler in their design than the parish church because chapels were built 'at one go', while churches have been altered over long periods of time during which bits and pieces have been added to them. Unfortunately, over the last few years a lot of chapels have been pulled down and the land they stood on sold for development. At the same time other chapels have been converted to non-religious uses, because fewer people are using them for their original purpose.

The Old Baptist Chapel at Tewkesbury in Gloucestershire dates from the seventeenth century and is one of the oldest surviving chapels. Look at this picture of the inside. You can see how very different it is from the interior of a church. At Fressingfield in Suffolk, the Strict Baptist Chapel, built in 1835, is coffin-shaped!

10 Defence – forts and battles

It is more than two hundred years since the last battle fought on British soil took place at Culloden in 1746. Before that date there had been much military activity through the centuries, and traces of it are easy to find.

The Romans, who landed here in 43 A.D. and stayed for nearly four hundred years, were the first to leave the mark of their army on the countryside, particularly in the building of roads, fortresses and fortifications. Of course, the earlier inhabitants of the country had not been exactly peaceful. Tribe fought against tribe over many years, but there is now no trace of this bloodthirsty warfare. The so-called 'forts' and 'camps' built by prehistoric man were not really anything to do with soldiers or warriors at all, as we have seen in Chapter 2. So we begin with the Romans.

The most impressive remains of the Roman army are in the north of England. This part of the country was a frontier of the Roman Empire and was heavily fortified. Right across England from Bowness-on-Solway in the west to Wallsend-on-Tyne in the east, a distance of 117 kilometres, stretches Hadrian's Wall.

Hadrian's Wall

It was built in the second century A.D. to protect Roman territory and to control traffic north and south, rather like the way in which modern customs posts now control movement between countries. At the southern gateway to Housesteads Fort in Northumberland you can still see the grooves made by cart and chariot wheels in the worn-down stone.

The Wall was built over a great period of time, and long stretches of it have survived. Built of stone, it was intended to be ten feet thick and fifteen feet high (about 3 m × 4·5 m), but was in fact completed on a smaller scale. There were fortifications called turrets and milecastles along its length, where soldiers on duty watching the frontier could shelter and defend

Gateway, Housesteads Fort

themselves from attack by northern tribes. The Northumberland town of Corbridge (Corstopitum to the Romans) was the central depot from which troops were supplied with food and equipment, and there were also large forts just behind the Wall where regiments were stationed. At Housesteads there are the remains of an infantry fort, and at Chesters, a few kilometres to the east, a cavalry one.

The Roman army moved into Scotland, and although its conquest was never completed they did build the Antonine Wall much further north. It can be traced for most of its length, although what remains of it has to be looked for near factories, suburban gardens and golf courses. At New Kilpatrick in Strathclyde, for example, there is a cemetery on a hillside. Between the graves can be seen a section of the foundations of the Antonine Wall, measuring about 38 cm across. There is another section at Camelon, near Falkirk, but generally the Antonine Wall is not as interesting to see as Hadrian's Wall.

Because of the importance of the frontier region near Hadrian's Wall there is a lot to see in the area. Excavations by archaeologists are still going on, and there have been some exciting discoveries recently at Vindolanda in Northumberland, one of the major settlements. You may need some help if you don't want to miss anything, and there is an excellent short guide to Hadrian's Wall published by the Department of the Environment, which is responsible for looking after these historic areas. It tells you which parts of the Wall can be visited, when they are open to the public and how much the admission charge is.

Here are some examples of other military remains to look out for. At Caerleon in Wales you can see the remains of a barracks where a Roman legion was stationed. In London, near the Tower, there is a piece of the wall which used to protect the Roman town of Londinium; and at Caerwent in Wales a longer stretch of the town wall survives.

The Romans seem to have been everywhere in this country – and so they were. Their army has even left its mark on our language. The word 'century' came from the Roman 'century'

Roman barracks at Caerleon, Wales

Roman wall, London

which was a unit of 80 (not 100!) soldiers commanded by a centurion.

The Romans built a number of forts around the east coast of Britain. They had crossed the channel as invaders, and were concerned that Saxon tribes who were not part of their empire should not be able to do the same thing! The sites of nine of these forts are known today. They were under the command of an officer called The Count of the Saxon Shore, and his job was to keep invaders out. The map overleaf shows that all these forts are on or near the sea, guarding the harbours or river mouths that any invading force would have to use. This part of the coast has always been attractive to would-be invaders because it is so close to the continent of Europe. William the Conqueror

came this way and Napoleon and Hitler both thought about doing so – if their invasions had taken place, this is the route they would have chosen.

Nothing much remains of Brancaster fort in Norfolk, but excavations have shown that it covered an area of just over 2.5 hectares, and its walls were about 2.75 metres thick. The next fort along the coast, going south, is at Burgh in Suffolk. This is much better preserved. Today it stands by the River Waveney, but the coastline has changed since Roman times, when it was much nearer the sea.

There are remains to be seen at Bradwell in Essex too, while at Reculver in Kent the sea has eaten away nearly half the Roman fort. At Richborough the sea used to lap against the walls of the fort, which now stands isolated on a small hill overlooking fields. One side of the fort has collapsed. In Roman times the hill on which its ruins stand was an island. Together with Hadrian's Wall, Richborough is the most important military monument in Britain.

The fort at Dover is buried underneath the modern town, but a Roman lighthouse still stands in the courtyard of Dover castle. (The castle was built in the middle ages, long after the Romans had left.) At Lympne only a few walls of the fort are left, almost lost in the wastes of Romney Marsh.

The last two forts of the Saxon Shore are at Pevensey in Sussex and Portchester in Hampshire. They are especially interesting because six centuries later the Normans built castles within the walls of the Roman ones. To visit Pevensey or Portchester today is exciting. Here you can really feel the presence of the Roman soldiers who constructed the original forts, and see just how solidly they built. Their walls are more lasting than the Norman ones!

The Normans, led by William the Conqueror, invaded this country in 1066. They were great castle builders, and castles were the strongholds which gave security to the victorious Normans in a land where the population was hostile to them. Within the castle walls the baron or lord lived a normal life with his family, his servants and his soldiers; and it was from here that he ruled the land which William had given him.

When we speak of living a normal life within the castles, however, we must remember that they were pretty uncomfortable places to live in, with stone floors, damp, inadequate heating and lack of privacy. As the knights who had gone abroad on Crusades brought home with them from the Middle East all sorts of ideas about comfort in the home, they must have wondered about the advantages of castle life in Britain! But there were more obvious reasons why castles eventually went out of use. They had been built mainly for military purposes, and as the country became more settled so there was less need

Roman lighthouse, Dover Castle

for protection. In addition, as the science of artillery developed, castle walls were no defence against big guns.

Many of the ruined castles that you see today were deliberately destroyed by Oliver Cromwell's Parliamentary soldiers in the Civil War, to prevent their being used by supporters of the King. Others simply fell out of use and the stone from which they were built was taken away by local people to build and repair their own homes. A good example of this is at Bramber in Sussex, where very little remains of the castle on the hill – while the village below has some fine stone-built houses!

There is no such thing as a typical castle. They were built on an individual pattern according to the lie of the land. Some of the features you can look for are these:

MOTTE – earth mound upon which the first buildings were erected;
BAILEY or WARD – the space within the outer defences;
CURTAIN WALL – enclosing wall, with towers for defence;
KEEP – the strongpoint of the castle;
GATEHOUSE – main entrance, a gateway with towers.

You may also find a moat or ditch surrounding the castle, and slits in the walls through which arrows could be fired at an attacking enemy.

The plan of the Tower of London on the opposite page shows how one castle developed.

When it was first built in 1080, the Tower consisted of a keep (now called the White Tower) and an inner bailey between the tower and the River Thames. The walls of the bailey were put up in 1097, and the middle bailey was added in about 1190. Rebuilding took place in the thirteenth century when the outer bailey, its walls and a moat were added. If you visit the Tower of London today, there is so much to see that there are guides, called yeoman warders, who will point out things of interest and answer your questions. The uniform they wear dates from the reign of Henry VIII, and you should never call them 'beefeaters'!

Durham Castle, which was begun in 1072, is a different shape, altered and rebuilt over the centuries.

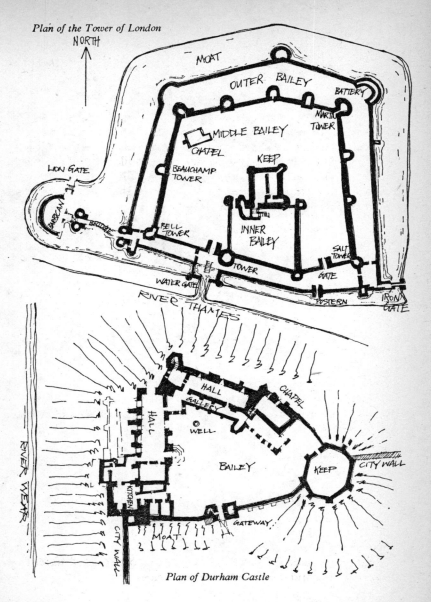

Plan of the Tower of London

NORTH

MOAT

OUTER BAILEY

BATTERY

MARTIN TOWER

MIDDLE BAILEY

CHAPEL

KEEP

BEAUCHAMP TOWER

LION GATE

BARBICAN

BRIDGE

BELL TOWER

INNER BAILEY

SALT TOWER

WATER GATE

TOWER

GATE

POSTERN

IRON GATE

RIVER THAMES

HALL

CHAPEL

GALLERY

HALL

WELL

RIVER WEAR

BAILEY

KEEP

CITY WALL

KITCHEN

GATEWAY

CITY WALL

MOAT

Plan of Durham Castle

Corfe Castle, Dorset

City wall, Canterbury, Kent

A Martello tower

Tonbridge Castle in Kent is much simpler in design. Today you can see the ruined keep, the gatehouse and part of the curtain wall.

Bamburgh Castle, on the north-east coast about eighty kilometres from Newcastle upon Tyne, is open to visitors. It has been completely restored, and broods over the sea and the countryside as it has done for more than eight centuries.

Corfe Castle in Dorset is beautifully set in a gap of the Purbeck Hills, and you can see when you visit it how the castle dominated the land around it before it was destroyed by Cromwell's soldiers in 1646. The ruined towers and blocks are a reminder of violence and death in this quiet landscape.

Look again at the plan of Durham Castle, and you will see where the city wall joins it. Protective walls like this were built in unsettled times round old towns and cities, and where they have survived they are well worth seeing today. At Canterbury in Kent, a long stretch of the wall is still standing; and so is the Westgate, which was built in 1380 to control traffic in and out of the city, and to bar the way to unwelcome visitors. Later it became the city gaol and served this purpose till 1829, and now it is a museum.

At the beginning of the nineteenth century, when an invasion by Napoleon was feared, one hundred and three small forts, called Martello Towers, were built around the coast from Suffolk to Sussex. Each one held a small garrison of soldiers, who entered it by means of a ladder to a door just over six metres from the ground. The towers were never used, because no invasion took place; and although most of them have been pulled down, some still stand by the sea. Near Dymchurch in Kent there is one which has been turned into a museum.

More than fifty battles have taken place in Britain, and there is something very special about visiting an old battlefield. Don't be put off if somebody tells you, 'There's nothing to see here now.' There is always something to be seen if you look hard enough – maybe a slope down which cavalry charged, or a rusty sword hanging in a nearby church. Even where a town now covers a battlefield, as at St Albans in Hertfordshire, it is still possible to trace the course of the action. On the wall of the

National Westminster Bank in St Albans hangs a plaque recording the death of the Duke of Somerset (a leading officer in the battle) near that spot; and around the market-place the layout of the streets is identical with what it was when the battle took place in 1455.

The Battle of Rottingdean took place in 1377, when a band of French pirates landed on the Sussex coast and advanced on the village. Several of the inhabitants took refuge in the belfry of the church. The pirates set fire to it, and next day a battle was fought. Both sides lost heavily, and the pirates went back to their ships taking some prisoners with them. Those who had tried to find shelter in the church were killed, and all signs of the fighting have disappeared except in the church, where scorch marks can still be seen on three of the four pillars supporting the tower and belfry.

If you visit a battlefield it is a good idea to know something about why the battle was fought, and to take with you a plan of how the soldiers on both sides were placed before the action. The best book I know for this is *Battles and Battlefields* by David Scott Daniell, published by Beaver Books. The background information, the maps and the pictures in it are very clear.

Take the Battle of Naseby (1645), for instance. Here the battlefield looks almost the same today as it did over three hundred years ago. There are more hedges, but by walking round you can trace where the fighting took place, and you can walk down Sulby Hedge where Colonel Okey's dragoons fired their muskets at the attacking royalists. The village of Naseby in Northamptonshire is a sleepy little place. The church contains some relics of the battle, but there is not much else to suggest that the most important battle of the English Civil War was fought nearby. It is the battlefield itself which has the real atmosphere of the past.

It is an odd fact that if you want to see what an eighteenth-century barracks for soldiers looked like, you have to go to Halifax in Nova Scotia, or to another of the places in Canada or the United States where old military installations have been beautifully restored as an attraction for visitors. The reason for

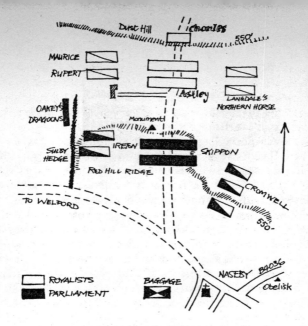

Plan of the Battle of Naseby, 1645

this is that when the British Army went abroad in the eighteenth century, it had to build its own quarters, whereas in this country soldiers were billeted in public houses and in private homes. Barracks were not built until the time of Queen Victoria. Places like Aldershot (Hampshire) and Colchester (Essex) became garrison towns, but both have been extensively rebuilt in recent years, so that little remains of the past.

There were also barracks in many of our towns, but those which still exist today have been modernised and made much more comfortable to live in. On the other hand, the strength of the Army has declined since the end of the Second World War, and so many of these barracks have fallen into disuse. But some reminders of the past have survived, like this imposing entrance to Fulwood Barracks at Preston in Lancashire; and at Dorchester in Dorset part of the old barracks is now used as a military museum.

At Monmouth in Wales you can still see a fortified bridge, which is more than seven hundred years old. It was built both to let traffic cross the river and to protect the town. Just over the archway you will see a stonework projection, and from here boiling oil or pitch could be poured onto the heads of the attackers below! There is one other fortified bridge, at Warkworth in Northumberland.

Most towns and villages have war memorials, and so do many churches. They are a reminder of past wars, especially the World Wars of 1914–18 and 1939–45. Right in the middle of England at Meriden, Warwickshire, there is this memorial which reads: 'In Remembrance of Those CYCLISTS Who Gave Their Lives in World War I, 1914–1918'.

Finally, two other small wartime reminders. You may come across pill-boxes from the Second World War. These are small concrete forts, built at a time when there was fear of a German parachute invasion; and if you are interested in naval matters, *HMS Victory* at Portsmouth, flagship of Admiral Lord Nelson, gives the best idea of how sailors lived and died in Britain's naval past.

Fortified bridge, Monmouth, Wales

11 Industry

This flint mine on Blackpatch Hill near Findon in Sussex was being used in prehistoric times, so you will see that mining is a very old industry. It is also an industry which has left very definite marks on the countryside.

Flint mine, Blackpatch Hill, Sussex

Coal has been dug out of the earth for hundreds of years, and the sight of a coal mine with its winding gear, railway wagons, coal heaps and cluster of buildings reminds us that we have depended a great deal on coal in the past, and continue to do so today. Miners have a very difficult and dangerous job to do, but it has been possible to provide better working conditions now for some of them than they used to have. This retired Northumberland miner, Norman Thompson, remembers what things were like when he began work fifty years ago:

'There were no Pithead Baths then, and we had to use the big bath-tub on the kitchen floor, until baths were installed in the homes, or at the Pits. This was part of the scene when I first started the Pits.'

He remembers the happier side of things as well:

'The older workmen used to play the usual tricks on the new starters, and I was told one day to go to the Black-smith's Shop for a capful of nail-holes. On the way to the shop, I kept asking myself, what was a capful of nail-holes, but I gave it up. When I saw the blacksmith I told him what I had come for. He looked at me once, then took my hat off, went across to his anvil, picked up his hammer and punch, and filled my hat with holes! "There's your capful of nail-holes," he said, quite serious, with never a smile.'

If somebody said to you that eight pigs made a fother, would you know what they meant? Probably not, because this is the language once used by lead miners in the Peak District of Derbyshire. This ancient industry has now vanished, but the few old buildings and mineshafts which remain are worth see-ing because the miners used local materials, and they blend in beautifully with the surrounding countryside. But a word of warning: if you are in this area, be very careful because open mineshafts may be hidden in long grass, and heaps of stone are not always safe. You really should not explore lead-mining country without a grown-up.

These pictures show a lead mine and a mine shaft with ging-ing. 'Ginging'? Like 'pig' and 'fother', this is a lead-mining word, and the ginging you see in the picture is the dressed stone work round the edge, holding up the loose ground and prevent-ing it from falling into the mine. A pig is a block of cast lead, and eight of them made a fother, weighing about 1134 kilos.

Tin has been mined in Cornwall since prehistoric times, and from 1800 to 1850 it was a flourishing industry. This is not so today, but there are many remains of old mines and their buildings. Some, without roofs or windows, are quietly decay-ing; others are preserved as ancient monuments; and a few

Lead mine, Peak District, Derbyshire

A mine shaft with ginging

Ruined engine
houses and stacks,
Cornwall

115

buildings have been converted into private houses. Near St
Cleer is a deserted mining village. However, these ruined engine
houses and stacks are more typical of what you can see in
Cornwall, shown on page 115, helping you to imagine the
noise and bustle of a tin mine working.

The china-clay industry is still alive in Cornwall, and pro-
duces great heaps of waste like those near St Austell. Nothing
will grow on these heaps, and because the land is covered with
this gleaming but dead matter it is hard to think that it will ever
have any interest for anyone.

Of course, industry does not have to spoil the countryside.
Gloucestershire was once the centre of the wool trade, and even
today there are still hundreds of mills to be seen, some in ruins,
others in good shape. Shown above is New Mills, Wotton-
under-Edge, sitting beside the mill pond which supplied it with
power. Look at it closely, because there is something unusual
about it . . . it is in fact a brick building in an area where local
stone is much more widely used than brick for building, and is a
special feature of the Cotswolds, as this part of the country is

called. Visit the Cotswolds if you can, for many old mills are situated in towns like Wotton-under-Edge or Stroud, and years ago, when wool was produced and exported in huge quantities, it was in towns such as these, with their many beautiful buildings, that most of England's wealth was created. As a reminder of those far-off times when wool was so important, the Lord Chancellor in the House of Lords still sits on the woolsack – a sack of wool covered in scarlet.

In Uttoxeter Road, Longton, Staffordshire, the Gladstone Pottery has been preserved as an industrial museum, and here you can see just how pots for household use were made a hundred years ago. Among the raw materials required were flint and bone which had to be ground down before the potters could use them. Just beside the Trent and Mersey Canal, close to the junction with the Caldon Canal, stands the Etruscan Bone and Flint Mill – a wonderful example of an old industrial building, and a reminder, too, of how important canals were for carrying goods in bulk.

At Blaenavon in South Wales the remains of the ironworks founded in 1789 give us a much wilder picture, as you can see. The stone walls of the furnaces have crumbled away, but the brickwork and the iron bands which were used to strengthen them are still there.

Ironworks at Blaenavon, South Wales

The first cast iron bridge, Ironbridge, Shropshire

The first cast iron bridge in the world was erected at Ironbridge, Shropshire, in 1779. The man responsible for its building was Abraham Darby, whose grandfather (also named Abraham) had been the first man to make a success of smelting iron with coke. This process made possible the large-scale production of iron, without which the development of modern industry would have been impossible.

The site where the Darby family worked, at Coalbrookdale in the Severn Gorge, was exactly right for its purpose. Coal and iron ore were close by, and there was water power for the bellows which were used to make the high temperatures needed in the furnaces. Then there was the closeness of the River Severn, one of the busiest routes in the eighteenth century, so that goods could be moved easily to distant markets.

Besides the first cast iron bridge, the first iron railway track was made here, and by a stroke of luck most of the places in Coalbrookdale where all this engineering and manufacture went on have survived. The Ironbridge Gorge Museum Trust has been rediscovering, and quite literally unearthing, canals, furnaces, warehouses, tunnels, engines, etc., scattered over more than fifteen square kilometres of the valley.

There is still a lot of work to be done, but the whole area is

Cast iron chimneys

Cast iron clock

already very exciting and easy to explore, with clear 'information points' here and there to help you, and a 'park and ride' scheme so that you don't have to tour by car. The entrance fee as I write is £1, which may seem high, but there are several museums, and you will need a whole day to get round everything. This above all is a part of Britain where you can get the feel of industry in the past, and sense how it must have changed the landscape and the lives of people.

Amongst some of the things you may notice are the unusual cast iron chimneys on a cottage near the entrance to the works museum. Then there is the marvellous Great Warehouse, built in 1830, with a cast iron clock which was added later. Even the window frames and window sills are made of iron! Turn back one page for pictures of the chimneys and clock. .

Haystack boiler

But the most striking things to be seen are the old furnace, parts of which date from 1638, and the 'haystack' boiler which is 250 years old. These relics are the best possible reminder of the history of industry.

Nevertheless, you don't have to go to Coalbrookdale to find such reminders. They are all around you. Factories, power stations, roads, railways and canals are all part of our industrial history. The garage where petrol is sold and where motor cars are repaired is a modern version of stables where horses were looked after and coaches were kept. And already somebody is writing the history of airports!

One of the results of the growth of industry since 1801 has been that more and more people left the countryside and came to live and work in towns, where jobs were easier to get and better paid. This changeover from country work to industrial work and town living is called the 'Industrial Revolution', and it caused great problems, especially as most people had never lived and worked amongst large numbers of their fellow men and women before.

An engineer named Thomas Wood, born in 1822, went to work at a large machine shop in Oldham (now part of Greater Manchester). He was nervous when he started, for the firm employed two thousand workmen and he had never worked before with more than eight or ten men. 'It was with fear that I commenced work...,' he said; but because he was hardworking and adaptable he put up with it, and so did most people who left behind the life which was familiar to them, and went to earn their living in factories.

When you look at the relics of industry, remember people like Thomas Wood. They have not left any memorials, but they did the laborious jobs, the fetching and the carrying, the operation of the machines. Men such as Abraham Darby had the ideas, but it was their workers who put them into practice.

See also :   5 Towns and Cities
       7 Transport

Britain's urban/rural population balance, 1801–1951

12 Law and order

In days gone by, before there was an organised police force, an elected constable was responsible for keeping law and order in each village or parish. Anyone accused of an offence would be arrested and taken before the local justice of the peace – a kind of magistrate. In trivial cases he would order punishment of the offender then and there or release him if judged innocent. Those accused of more serious crimes would be sent to the nearest town to await trial by judge and jury.

A court in which trials of this kind took place can be seen at Dorchester in Dorset. Here the Old Crown Court is preserved in a building which is now used for local council offices, and is open to visitors. It was built in 1796–97 on the site of a much older court, and remained in use until 1955. Underneath it are the cells where prisoners were kept while awaiting trial. They are dark and cheerless. One prisoner, George Loveless, wrote

Old Crown Court, Dorchester, Dorset

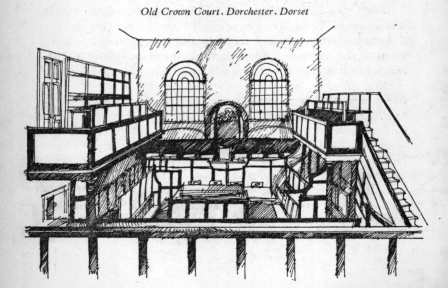

of them in 1834: 'To make it more disagreeable some wet and green brushwood was served for firing. The smoke of this place, together with its natural dampness, amounted to nearly suffocation, and in this dreadful situation we passed three whole days.'

Another gruesome reminder of the past is the condemned cell in York Castle, now part of the Museum. Prisoners who were to be hanged were kept here, and the best known occupant of this cell was Dick Turpin, the highwayman, who was hanged in York in 1739.

Condemned cell, York Castle

Hanging was the punishment for a wide range of crimes. Even stealing a sheep, or goods to the value of more than five shillings, once carried the death penalty. Execution was carried out in public as a warning to others who might be tempted into a life of crime. Sometimes, too, the body of a hanged man would be taken to a spot near the scene of the crime and left there hanging from a gibbet until it rotted away, as a dreadful warning. A gibbet used for this purpose still stands near Elsdon in Northumberland on the B6341 road, at a place called Steng Cross (see overleaf). Travellers passing by in 1791 would have seen the body of William Winter hanging in irons. He had been put to death at York for the murder of an old woman named Margaret Crozier. You can also see a set of gibbet irons at the Town Hall in Rye, Sussex.

Execution block, Tower Hill

Gibbet at Steng Cross, Northumberland

In the Tower of London various dungeons are open to the public, and there are torture implements such as the rack which was used to make Guy Fawkes betray his companions in the Gunpowder Plot. You can also see the block and axe used for executions by beheading on Tower Hill.

Other relics of law and order are not quite so gruesome! In villages and small towns you may still find a building which served as the local lock-up – sometimes called a cage, blind house or Lob's pound. This was where the constable kept his prisoners before they appeared in front of the justice of the peace, or before they were taken elsewhere for trial. Drunks would be put in the lock-up until they were sober, and anyone who disturbed the peace was likely to end up in this small, dark and uncomfortable prison for a few hours.

At Walsingham, Norfolk, there is a lock-up which also served as a beacon, as you can see in this picture; while at Anstey in Hertfordshire the lych-gate of St George's Church had the village cage built into it.

Lock-up at Walsingham, Norfolk

Lock-ups have now moved into the police station, but another form of local punishment which was very common indeed went out of use altogether in the 1830s. You may guess that we are now thinking of the stocks. These had been around since the fourteenth century, and an Act of 1405 laid down that they should be provided in every town and village. A wrong-doer might have to sit in the stocks (a wooden frame with holes for hands and feet) for up to four hours at a time, as a punishment for crimes like drunkenness, blasphemy, or even playing games on Sunday! Sometimes, too, a beggar would be put in the stocks before being driven out of the village. It was a cheap way of punishing people – the local carpenter and blacksmith could build a set of stocks very easily – and it had the great advantage of providing punishment in public, so that justice could be seen to be done as a warning to others.

Sometimes stocks were equipped with handcuffs, so that they could double as a whipping post. Whipping was another common punishment. As a poet named John Taylor put it in the seventeenth century:

'In London, and within a mile, I ween,
There are jails or prisons full eighteen,
And sixty whipping-posts, and stocks and cages.'

Stocks near Leigh, Kent

Apart from stocks and whipping, there was another way of punishing dishonest tradesmen, nagging wives and quarrelsome people – they were quite literally 'cooled off' by means of the ducking stool. This consisted of a chair attached to a

A ducking stool, Herefordshire

long beam, which swung on a pivot at the edge of the village pond. The offender could then be tied into the chair and lowered into the water by means of the beam. Sometimes the ducking stool was mounted on wheels, like this one in Leominster Priory Church, Herefordshire, so that the victim could be tied in place and wheeled round the village to be jeered at before the ducking took place. This particular stool was last used in 1817, although on that occasion sentence could not be carried out properly because at the time there was no water in the pond!

Like the stocks, the ducking stool provided a cheap and public way of punishing folk who offended against their fellow villagers. There is a record, for instance, that a new ducking stool was ordered at Bilston, Staffordshire, in 1695. Its cost was ten shillings (50 pence in today's money!).

Last of all, the department of dreadful warnings. On several bridges in Dorset you can see a metal notice like the one below.

To be transported was a terrible punishment. Men and women who suffered this sentence were sent in chains to convict settlements in Australia, so the notice is a reminder of a very much more harsh way of life in the past.

A warning notice in Dorset

> **· DORSET ·**
> ANY PERSON WILFULLY INJURING
> ANY PART OF THIS COUNTY BRIDGE
> WILL BE GUILTY OF FELONY AND
> UPON CONVICTION LIABLE TO BE
> **TRANSPORTED FOR LIFE**
> BY THE COURT
> 7 & 8 GEO 4 C 30 S 13   T FOOKS

13 Government

Probably the best-known government building in the country is London's Palace of Westminster, more often referred to as the Houses of Parliament, where the House of Commons and the House of Lords meet. From the clock tower Big Ben strikes the hours with its famous chimes, and from the same tower a light shines whenever Parliament is sitting at night.

The Houses of Parliament

The palace was first built for King Edward the Confessor, and kings of England lived there until the reign of Henry VIII. During those years when it was a royal home, all kinds of additions and alterations were made to the building – and things did not always go smoothly! More than six hundred years ago, in 1331, there was a strike of stonemasons working there. They would not work 'on Monday or Tuesday, because they were in arrear of their wages since Christmas and they thought they would lose those wages, until the Lord Treasurer promised that they should be fully paid for time past and future, and then they began to work on Wednesday,' says an old document.

Much more damaging than the strike was the fire which broke out in 1512. King Henry VIII moved out and the palace at Westminster was abandoned as a home for kings and queens. In 1547 Edward VI granted the use of the chapel of St Stephen to the House of Commons, who until then had met in one of the buildings belonging to Westminster Abbey. The Commons stayed here until 1834, when there was another fire which destroyed everything on the site except for Westminster Hall, the crypt of St Stephen's Chapel and the cloisters.

Six years later, in 1840, work was begun on a new Palace of Westminster, and in 1852 the splendid new buildings were opened with great ceremony by Queen Victoria. They remained in use until 1941, when they suffered damage from wartime bombing, and after the war they were again rebuilt and formally opened in 1950.

There is a public entrance for visitors in Old Palace Yard. The Yard itself lies between the Houses of Parliament and Westminster Abbey, and is on the site of the inner court of the palace built for King Edward the Confessor. Later it became a place of execution – Sir Walter Raleigh and Guy Fawkes were put to death here.

Westminster Hall, close by, was built for King William II between 1077 and 1079 as a banqueting hall for the palace. Luckily it escaped damage by fire and bombing. The enormous roof, unsupported by pillars, is a wonderful sight, and it was in this hall that Charles I was tried in 1649 before his execution in Whitehall. Guy Fawkes was tried here too.

Other palaces were built for kings and queens and are still in use as royal residences. Buckingham Palace is the Queen's London home, and thousands of visitors go each year to watch the changing of the guard. The palace stands on land which was planted about three hundred years ago with 30,000 mulberry trees. The idea was to have a British silk industry, and the leaves

Westminster Hall

were intended as food for the silkworms. Unfortunately, black mulberries were planted instead of the white ones which the worms liked to feed upon, and the experiment was not successful, although one famous English poet, John Dryden, was very fond of the mulberry tarts which were made nearby! The land was then built upon, and shortly after he became King, George III bought Buckingham House as a country retreat for himself and his wife. Thus in 1775 it was called 'The Queen's House', and throughout several reigns it was enlarged to become a 'palace'. When Queen Victoria lived there she really did not like its appearance, and complained once that it was 'a disgrace' (heavily underlined!), while someone else was known to suggest that the best thing would be for Aladdin to rub his magic lamp and shift the whole thing to a desert in Africa. None of this, however, has prevented Buckingham Palace from becoming one of the most popular sights in London.

St James's Palace, where the Queen Mother now lives, looks much more like a real palace, although no reigning king or queen has lived in it since the time of George III. About a thousand years ago there was a leper hospital here. By the time Henry VIII became king it housed only one old man and three old women, each of them receiving £2.60 and a quarter barrel of beer each year. Henry found them somewhere else to go, and had a hunting lodge built for Anne Boleyn on the site. On every possible surface he had the initials 'H' and 'A' carved – and you can still see these letters today – but after Queen Anne Boleyn's head had been chopped off by his orders, King Henry did not often go there again!

By the time George II became king the building, now known as St James's Palace, was fully used by the royal family, and it was possible to buy a ticket for the public enclosure from which people could watch the king and his family eating their Sunday dinner!

The Queen's Scottish home is at Balmoral, and it was built for Queen Victoria. In 1852 a strange miser, John Camden Nield, died and left the queen a quarter of a million pounds. She was puzzled as to why he had done this, but had no doubts about how to spend the money. She bought the Balmoral estate, had the old house pulled down, and replaced it by the one which is still in use today.

The strangest royal house is the Pavilion at Brighton, built in the style of an eastern palace, at a cost of over half a million pounds, for George IV when he was Prince Regent. He spent quite a lot of time there; but Queen Victoria did not like it at all, and in 1849 the Pavilion was sold to the town of Brighton after 143 vanloads of furniture had been removed and distributed to other royal palaces. Today the buildings are open to visitors, and during the First World War they were used as a hospital for wounded Indian soldiers.

Several other buildings have royal connections or royal histories, for example Kensington Palace, Windsor Castle, Holyrood Palace in Scotland, Sandringham House in Norfolk, Osborne House on the Isle of Wight and Hampton Court Palace. Most of them are reminders of times when kings and queens played a much more powerful role in government than they do today.

Buckingham Palace

St James's Palace

The Royal Pavilion, Brighton

Government buildings are found everywhere. Post offices can be numbered amongst these, and though most of them are now in modern premises you may come across older buildings like this postman's sorting office at Highgate in North London.

G.P.O. sorting office, Highgate

Similarly, while more and more government departments are housed in large modern office blocks especially built to hold the many civil servants who carry out the day-to-day running of the country's affairs, some old official buildings remain. One of the finest is the Customs House at King's Lynn in Norfolk. It was built in 1683, and in a recess in the lantern tower right at the top of the building is a statue of King Charles II. This town was the only one in East Anglia which remained loyal to him.

Although it is not, strictly speaking, a government building, the Corn Exchange was a feature of many towns in the past.

Custom's House, King's Lynn, Norfolk

Corn Exchange,
Newbury, Berkshire

Market hall, Ross-on-Wye, Herefordshire

Moot hall, Aldeburgh, Suffolk

Guild Hall, Winchester, Hampshire

135

Here corn was bought and sold, and because the towns often depended for their livelihood on such business, the Corn Exchange was likely to have a very prominent place. The one at Newbury in Berkshire was built in 1861.

Laws are made in Parliament, but from early times in this country such problems as maintaining roads and bridges, looking after the poor, running markets, dealing with law-breakers and providing schools have been left as the responsibility of men and women on the spot. These are some of the things which local government has been concerned with, and there has always been a changing balance between local government and the authority of Parliament.

Local men – and, much later, women – have been meeting together to discuss problems and plans for more than a thousand years, and the town hall that you see today is descended from the market hall, sometimes called a guildhall, where they met. There is a picture on page 46 of the guildhall at Thaxted in Essex, under which the market was held. On page 134 is a market hall built in 1670 in Ross-on-Wye, Herefordshire. It stands on fourteen pillars, and has a clock with four faces on its roof.

Other local assemblies took place in moot halls, of which the one built over four hundred years ago in Aldeburgh, Suffolk (pictured on page 135), is a good example.

As towns grew larger in the nineteenth century, so guildhalls, market halls and moot halls gave way to town halls, with a council chamber for elected councillors to meet in, and a 'Mayor's Parlour' for their leader. Sometimes, as at Winchester in Hampshire, the new town hall was given an old name. Turn back to page 135 to see a picture of the guildhall built in 1873 in the ancient city of Winchester. It is very imposing, and like so many nineteenth-century local government buildings, it symbolised the pride felt by people in their town and its achievements.

The smallest town hall in the country, by the way, is at Gatton Park in Surrey. The size of a summer house, it was built in 1765. A local landowner, Sir Roger Copley, decided to have it put up close to the door of his fine house. It is, of course, a curiosity, and not really able to serve as a town hall any more.

14 Street furniture

If you look at any busy road or street, you will see an assortment
of objects. Among them may be lamp-posts, road signs, pillar-
boxes, benches, notices, statues, memorials, traffic-lights,
telephone boxes, police boxes, bollards, railings, coal-hole
covers, clock towers, bus stops, fire hydrants, possibly drinking
fountains, and perhaps an occasional pump or horse trough. This
is what we call 'street furniture', and most of it was designed to
be useful. Statues, of course, had no direct use – they were
erected either as reminders of the great or to commemorate
someone who had made a special contribution to the local
community. In the same way there are memorials throughout
the country to the dead of this century's two World Wars, and
sometimes of earlier wars as well.

Some objects have outlived their usefulness. When it was
founded in 1859, the Metropolitan Drinking Fountain and
Cattle Trough Association started to put up drinking troughs

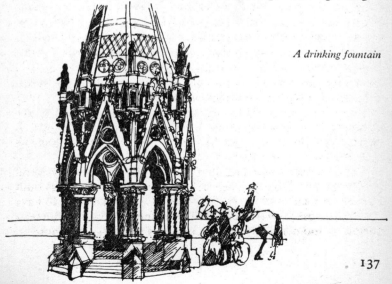

A drinking fountain

for horses. This was an act of kindness, and eventually there were 4600 of them; but since the motor car has now taken over from the horse as a means of transport, there is no need for these troughs, and most of them have been removed. Those which have survived are sometimes used for decoration, and flowers have been planted in them. The same Association also erected 2800 drinking fountains in an attempt to persuade people that water was better for them than cheap gin!

The commonest pieces of street furniture are road signs and lamp-posts. There are not many old signs left today. Until 1858 there were only milestones and guide posts, which I have talked about in Chapter 7; but in that year heavy steam engines and rollers were first used on the roads (and very heavy they were!) and so owners of bridges were allowed to put up notices warning drivers that the bridge would not take more than a certain weight. Such notices were made of cast iron, and you can still see them occasionally.

It was the cycling craze at the end of the nineteenth century that caused an increase in the number of road signs. Various cycling clubs put up signs from 1893, and by 1902, 32,000 had been erected all over the country. The first 'Steep Hill' warning was set up at the top of Muswell Hill in North London. But these early signs, and those which followed when motoring became popular in the early years of this century, have now almost all gone, so most of the signs that you see in your history hunting will be modern ones. A few old signs are tucked away in surprising places.

Shown opposite is an old street sign. Modern ones are stamped out of metal, and older ones are often made out of cast iron. You may come across an enamelled street sign with white lettering on a blue or green background. ARP signs are a reminder of the Second World War. 'ARP' stood for Air Raid Precautions, and the Warden was an official who took charge of shelter and rescue services during and after air raids. People needed to know where the Wardens could be found, and signs like the one shown opposite had a very useful job to do.

Finally, a very old sign which you can still see on older houses is a Fire Mark. In the eighteenth century, companies

A notice for drivers of heavy vehicles

A reminder of the Second World War

An old street sign

Some fire marks

who provided insurance against fire also ran a fire-fighting service, since this kind of protection was much cheaper than paying out money every time a house burned down! But of course the firemen would only deal with fires in buildings insured by their own company, so to avoid unnecessary expense, or the possibility of being cheated, the insurance company fixed signs to the houses they had agreed to protect. There were several insurance companies at the time, particularly in London; but if a householder was not insured with one of them, he could be very unlucky!

Lamp-posts are worth looking at. The first Act of Parliament to improve street lighting was passed in 1671, but the oldest lamp-posts still in use date from the nineteenth century. They

A selection of street lamps

A pillar-box dating from about 1853

are made of cast iron and look very ornamental. In London, on the Embankment and in Woburn Walk, there are some lovely examples of lamp-posts which fit in with their surroundings and provide good lighting at the same time. Sometimes street lamps were on a bracket which was then fixed to a wall.

We take pillar-boxes for granted, but they have quite a long history. They were used in Paris as far back as 1653, but the first one in England was an iron box fixed to the wall at Wakefield Post Office in West Yorkshire in 1809. In 1852 pillar-boxes were introduced in St Helier, Jersey, the Channel Islands, and three years later they came into use in London and spread quickly throughout the country. In 1858 the Post Office began using wall boxes, and in 1871 both kinds of letter-box were equipped with 'Hours of Collection' notices.

Above is an early pillar-box, from about 1853, still in use in a village called Bishop's Caundle in Dorset. You will see on every letter-box the mark of the king or queen in whose reign it was put up, and very often the maker's name too.

Traffic lights are also usually taken for granted – as long as they are working properly, we don't give them a second thought. While you won't see any old ones still in use, it is worth remembering that the earliest traffic signals were put up outside the Houses of Parliament in 1868, and worked by gas. Soon after they had come into use there was an explosion, and the policeman controlling them was killed – an accident which discouraged other experiments in traffic signals.

Modern traffic lights come from America, where they were first used in Cleveland, Ohio, in 1914. In 1925 there were traffic lights, controlled by a policeman, at the junction of St James's Street and Piccadilly in London. The first automatic traffic lights were used in Wolverhampton in the West Midlands in 1926.

In these days of nuclear power and oil, coal has remained a vital source of energy and heat for us all. Without coal we should never have become the leading industrial country in the world – a position that we held in the reign of Queen Victoria. This was a time when there was no alternative method of heating homes, and coal was often used for cooking-stoves as well. The job of digging coal by hand and bringing it to its users was an industry which employed many thousands of people. Today fewer people are involved, for some of the work is done by machinery, and in any case less coal is sold to householders.

There is a reminder of these great days of coal in the coal-hole covers, made of cast iron, which you can still see in the pavements of towns and cities. All the coalman did was to lift the cover and pour his coal into the cellar below – no need for him to tramp through the house with his sacks, leaving a trail of coal dust behind him. Many of these coal-hole covers were very carefully designed and attractive. Of course, some have been worn away as so many people have walked on them over the years, but there are still many to be seen.

On the road to Ware in Hertfordshire you can see a memorial stone. It is a monument to Thomas Clarkson, who worked for the abolition of slavery. In York, at the junction of Petergate and Minster Gates, there is a statue of Minerva, goddess of wisdom, sitting with a wise owl and a pile of books – a reminder of by-

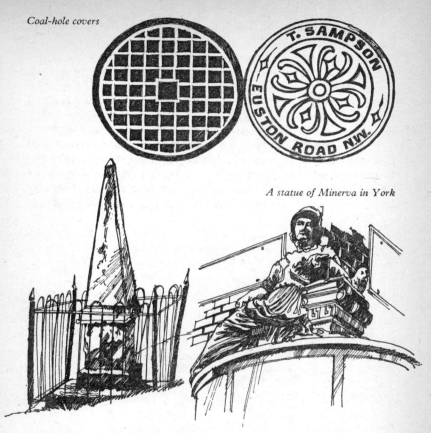

Coal-hole covers

T. SAMPSON
EUSTON ROAD N.W.

A statue of Minerva in York

Monument to Thomas Clarkson in Ware

gone York when booksellers and bookbinders had their shops here. Britain is rich in memorials and statues like these. They come in all shapes and sizes, and sometimes in places where you would least expect them.

Before piped water was brought into houses, water had to be taken from streams or springs or drawn from wells and pumps. At Aldworth in Berkshire there is a very deep well. It is no longer used, but with its roof and supporting timber it still looks very impressive. The strangest well in England is at Stoke Row in Oxfordshire. Built in 1863, it is called the Maharajah's Well, and the mechanism was so cleverly designed that even children were able to draw a nine-gallon bucketful of water (about 40 litres) from it. More than a hundred years ago a man from the village went out to India, and made friends there with the Maharajah of Benares. When the Maharajah was told that the village had no water supply he was surprised – so much so that he decided to pay for the construction of this well.

On the opposite page is the public pump at Aylesbury in Buckinghamshire, situated in a passageway running from Kingsbury to the church. Now it is just a relic of the past, no longer used, and bearing a notice which reads: 'Supplied the

A well at Aldworth, Berkshire

A well at Stoke Row, Oxfordshire

A *A pump at Aylesbury, Buckinghamshire*
B *A pump at Hemel Hempstead, Hertfordshire*
C *A telephone box in Tyneham, Dorset, partly hidden by a wall*

town's drinking water before the days of modern piped water. Installed about 1849.' The handle is a long way from the ground, so that there would have been steps to reach it.

A pump in the High Street of Hemel Hempstead in Hertfordshire has received unusual treatment. It has been converted into a street lamp, painted yellow, green and white, and is now a lovely piece of street furniture.

The telephone box shown above is in the village of Tyneham, Dorset. Because the village is part of an army training area nobody lives there now, and so this old box has survived. Compare it with those that you are used to seeing today.

15 Entertainment

People have always enjoyed entertainment. Long before there were any theatres, performances of singing, dancing and acting took place at any convenient spot where an audience could gather. The ancient Greeks built theatres in their own country where plays were acted; the Romans, too, built theatres, and the remains of one of them have been excavated at St Albans, not far from London. As you can see from this picture, it does not look much like the kind of theatre we are used to. Performances took place in the open air, and the audience sat round the arena where the action took place.

Roman theatre, Verulamium (St Albans)

After the Romans left, no theatres were built in this country for more than a thousand years. This does not mean that plays were not produced, nor that public entertainment went out of favour, for strolling players and minstrels wandered around performing in any available places, and religious plays were acted in churches and churchyards, and on carts which were drawn through cities like Chester or York so that the audience could, quite literally, follow the action of the play. This kind of entertainment, needless to say, has left no trace on the landscape, although a few plays have survived and have been printed, and there are one or two pictures of early performances.

In those days before theatres were built, actors sometimes gave performances in the courtyards and galleries of inns. They could be sure of an audience here, and the landlord would welcome the extra business they brought. One of these old inns with a gallery which could be used by actors has survived in London, and is shown in this picture of the George at Southwark.

The galleries at the George Inn, Southwark

The first London theatre was built for a man called James Burbage over four hundred years ago, in 1577. This was The Theatre, Shoreditch, whose site is marked today by a plaque on the buildings at 86–88 Curtain Road. Burbage was an actor and the manager of his theatre. Shortly after it had opened, he was ordered to close it during an outbreak of plague! He re-opened it later and the playhouse became a great success – the first of several to be built in the reign of Queen Elizabeth I.

Other London theatres which have now disappeared have their sites marked by a memorial plaque. There is one on the wall of the City of London School, John Carpenter Street, where the Duke's Theatre stood from 1671 to 1709. And at 225 Westminster Bridge Road a tablet put up in 1951 marks the site of one of London's most famous places of entertainment. This was Astley's Theatre, which became the Theatre Royal, Westminster, until it closed down in 1895. Philip Astley, the founder, had been a sergeant-major in the cavalry, and when he left the army in 1766 he looked round for a way to earn a living. He decided to open a riding school where people were invited to pay to see what went on. It proved popular, and so Astley added entertainment for their pleasure, with such attractions as daredevil riding, vaulting, balancing, tightrope walking, clowns – all the things that we associate today with the circus. When you see the ringmaster having a joky conversation with the clown during a performance, remember that this is a circus tradition which was started by Astley, and the place of entertainment which he founded in Westminster Bridge Road lasted for over a hundred years.

Astley was said to be very proud of his achievement, and there is a story that once when King George III was riding across Westminster Bridge his horse took fright at the sound of cheering. Astley was at hand to calm the animal, and the king asked him his name. 'Serjeant-Major Astley, Sire,' he replied, and went on: 'I am the owner of this here place for the exhibition of feats of activity on horseback.'

In King Street, Bristol, stands the Theatre Royal, built in 1766. It is the oldest surviving theatre in England. Many theatres were built during the eighteenth century, but most have either disappeared during the course of redevelopment or have been changed out of all recognition. In Brighton, for example, the Old Theatre building in Duke Street is now part of commercial premises. In Birmingham the Aston Hippodrome, which opened in 1908, closed as a theatre in 1961 and is now a bingo hall. Some theatres have become cinemas, for example the Theatre Royal in Blackpool, which is now the Tivoli Cinema. At Wakefield in Yorkshire the Royal Opera

Interior of the Theatre Royal, Bristol

House was opened in 1894 and remained as a theatre until 1954, when it was made into a cinema. This closed in 1966, and the building became a bingo hall, but you can still see the words ROYAL OPERA HOUSE carved in the stonework on the front of the building.

There is something sad about a theatre or cinema which is now derelict. At Bungay in Suffolk the New Theatre was opened in 1828. Later it became a corn exchange, a cinema, a skating rink, a laundry, and then a store; but some years ago it was 'To let', and looking very forlorn.

One of the oddest buildings connected with entertainment is the cinema in London's Islington which was built in the 1930s to look like an ancient Egyptian temple. Now a bingo hall, it still looks like a temple! (See page 150.)

Theatres . . . cinemas . . . and now television has taken over more and more of our entertainment. But television has a history too, and Alexandra Palace in North London, from which the first TV programmes were transmitted before war broke out in 1939, is still standing – although its future is uncertain.

1930s cinema, Islington

Seaside piers were built in the nineteenth century as an attraction for holiday-makers. A good many of them are still in use, although now, after a hundred years or so, some are in need of considerable repairs which are thought to be too costly to carry out. The pier at Southend in Essex is about two kilometres long, and has a railway running along it. Brighton in Sussex has two piers – the Palace Pier and the West Pier – and it was here that the first English pier was opened to the public in 1823. The Old Chain Pier was a landing point for the boat which went regularly from Brighton to Dieppe and back. It made life easier – and cheaper – for passengers, who had previously been rowed out to the boat in small craft or carried out on the shoulders of a longshoreman at a cost of three shillings, plus the certainty of getting their feet wet! This pier lasted until 1889, when it was sold for £15,000, complete with various additions such as a reading room, some small shops, and a wine and spirit store which was run by a couple whose daughter was to become famous as Ellen Terry, the actress. Seven years later, in 1896, the Old Chain Pier was washed away in a storm, and the Palace Pier was opened three years after that.

When you walk along a pier, you are on its 'deck' rather than the floor. It is this pretence of being at sea on a boat, but without the inconvenience of sea sickness or getting wet, that has made piers so attractive. With their shops, souvenir stalls and slot-machines, space for sitting in the sun with water almost all round you, and sometimes concert performances, they have certainly provided a great deal of entertainment.

Also look at the bandstand which is often as old as the pier. With its decorative ironwork, it is a reminder of the days when public concerts provided the popular music which is now more readily available on the radio and record player.

A seaside bandstand

A seaside pier

16 People in the past

About four hundred years ago a poet named Thomas Tusser wrote about people getting up in the morning:

'No sooner some up
But nose is in cup.'

Lots of us are like that: as soon as we get up we like to have a drink of something or other. In some ways people don't change – climbing out of bed on a cold morning is as horrid today as it was hundreds of years ago. People have always liked eating, drinking and enjoying themselves. So we can guess quite a bit about the way people behaved in the past; but a question for the history hunter to ask is: what did they look like?

Plenty of pictures can be found in books, and for the last hundred years or so there have been photographs; but you can also find what people looked like by studying church brasses, carvings, tombstones and statues.

Brasses, which you will find on tombstones inside churches, are flat carvings in metal, in memory of the deceased. Sometimes you will see a man and his wife together, or even a man who was married, widowed, and married again, so that he will be shown with two wives. At Writtle in Essex there is a brass, from about 1490, which shows an unknown man who had four wives, and they stand two on each side of him, with eighteen children as well!

The earliest known brass is of Sir John Daubernon (1277) in armour. It is over 1 m 82 cm high, and is in Stoke d'Abernon Church, Surrey.

At Felbrigg, Norfolk, there is another soldier with his wife. This is Sir Symon de Felbrygge, who carried Richard II's standard. He died in 1443, and his wife Margaret died twenty-seven years earlier in 1416.

These three men were the servants of Sir Charles Morrison

A brass of three servants, Parish church, Watford, Hertfordshire

at the beginning of the seventeenth century. Their names are Henry Dickson, George Miller and Anthony Cooper, and you can see them in the parish church of Watford in Hertfordshire.

Church brasses are worth looking for, and are one of the best ways of picturing the people who lived in the castles and old houses we have talked about.

You will also find carvings in churches, like the sixteenth-century clothworker carved in wood at Spaxton Church, Somerset.

Wood carving of a clothworker, Spaxton Church, Somerset

Outside in the churchyard, look for carved tombstones like the ones for farmer George Basey and his wife Ann at Ashby St Mary in Norfolk. Notice too that three of their grand-children died in infancy – a sad fact which reminds us that doctors were rare, or not very skilled, in those days, and hygiene not as well understood as it is today.

Likenesses of ordinary people are sometimes found in unexpected places. Richard Lenard was a Sussex ironfounder, and he can be seen, together with some of the implements he used in 1636, on a fireback made at his foundry. This is now in the Anne of Cleves House Museum at Lewes in Sussex.

Iron fireback showing Richard Lenard, a Sussex ironfounder

Most surprising of all are the series of carved pictures on an old dairy building at Stroud Green in North London. They show the progress of the milk from the farm until it is delivered to the customer. Here are two of the pictures; see for yourself how dress has changed in the last hundred years or so, and how the methods of milk delivery have altered – there were no milk bottles in those days, for example.

Murals outside the old dairy building at Stroud Green in North London

Milk delivery in town (above) and country (right)

18th-century boy,
St Bride's Church,
Fleet Street,
London

Sir Hugh Myddelton,
Islington Green, London

Statues can also tell us what people looked like. Not all of them portray kings, queens, famous soldiers and politicians. This statue of an eighteenth-century boy is in St Bride's Church, Fleet Street, London; and at Islington Green in London stands Sir Hugh Myddelton, famous for having brought piped water to London in the reign of Queen Elizabeth I. Perched on a memorial column at Wick Hill in Wiltshire sits Maud Heath, carrying a basket with eggs and poultry on her arm. A farmer's wife who lived five hundred years ago, she sold her produce in nearby Chippenham Market. In order to get there she had to cross a valley which was often flooded; and

A blue plaque on a London building

WILLIAM
BLIGH
1754 - 1817
COMMANDER
OF THE
BOUNTY
LIVED HERE

This stone obelisk, which stands at the eastern end of the causeway built by Maud Heath, is a second memorial to her

when she had made enough money, she had a raised pathway, or causeway, built so that other travellers from Wick Hill to Langley Burrell could cross the valley without getting their feet wet. The causeway is still in use today, and there she sits watching over it.

One last word: in London, houses where celebrated people lived are often marked with a blue plaque like this one. These commemorative tablets are worth looking out for. Of course they won't tell you anything about the appearance of people, but it helps our picture to know where some of the well-known people from the past lived.

17 How to go further in hunting for history

If you have followed me so far in the hunt for history, the chances are that you will want to go further. This little book is a beginning, but you cannot expect it to cover the place where you live, or where you may go on holiday or on a school outing. Here are some suggestions you can follow up.

I expect that you already belong to a public library. If you don't, then you should join one so that you will be able to borrow books. Two that you will find useful are *The Past we See Today*, which I wrote some years ago (published by Oxford University Press in 1972), and a book by Robert Dunning called *Local Sources for the Young Historian* (published by Frederick Muller in 1973). Ask the librarian if there are any other books of this sort, and ask too about the local history collection. It may not be kept at the branch of the library you use, but the librarian will tell you where you can see it. It will contain books, photographs, maps and other material relating to the way in which your part of the world has developed. The English, Welsh and Scottish Tourist Boards have joined together to publish an excellent sixteen-page booklet called *Discover Roman Britain*. It's full of maps, pictures and plans. If you can't get a copy in a local museum, write to the English Tourist Board at 4 Grosvenor Gardens, London SW1W 0DU.

It is also a good idea to make your own collection of guidebooks. A pleasant souvenir of a visit, they will remind you of what you have seen – or point out what you have missed! A very cheap series of paperbacks called the 'Discovering' books covers a whole range of subjects which you will find helpful, and these little books are brief, clearly written and well illustrated.

You should go to museums whenever you have the chance – I have mentioned one or two earlier in the book. They used to be pretty dull places, full of objects carefully tucked away in glass cases, but over the past few years things have changed a great deal, and displays are now much more exciting. Many outdoor museums have been set up, where you can look at houses, shops, machinery, transport and other things reconstructed with great care so that you can see just how people lived in the past. Amongst the excellent museums throughout the country, these four are first-class examples: the Museum of London covers the history of the capital, and at Beamish, Stanley in County Durham is the North of England Open Air Museum, where you can see the agricultural and industrial life of the area. I nearly said that this was the most fascinating of the new museums – but then I thought of the Welsh Folk Museum at St Fagans, near Cardiff, where the changing life and culture of the people of Wales can be seen. My special favourite is the Weald and Downland Open Air Museum at Singleton in Sussex. Here you can see several beautiful timber-framed buildings, and visit a charcoal-burner's camp.

The best thing about these four museums, and of course many others, is that they are not finished. Fresh displays and exhibits are always being added, and this gives the feeling of the past coming alive before your eyes.

We are much more concerned today than we used to be about saving old buildings and relics of the past. This is called 'conservation', and perhaps the period of tearing down old houses, factories, railway stations and so on is over. I hope it is.

The old house at Bocking in Essex shown in the front of the book was in a very bad state until Essex County Council bought it, modernised it, and sold it at a price which covered the cost of restoration. So a beautiful house is now preserved as a private home, and the atmosphere of the town has not been disturbed.

New discoveries about the past are always coming to light. Keep your eyes open! Good hunting!

More Beaver Books

We hope you have enjoyed this Beaver Book. Here are some of the other titles:

The Beaver Book of the Seaside A Beaver original. Snorkelling and surfing, birdwatching and beachcombing – plus facts about ships, lighthouses, smuggling, wrecks and lots of other fascinating topics. A book for everyone who loves the seaside by Jean Richardson; illustrated by Susan Neale and Peter Dennis

Exploring Nature A Beaver original. Make earthworms come at your command, learn the secret of the oak gall and discover how a fairy ring grows – just a few of the many exciting projects in this book for the budding naturalist. Written by Derek Hall and illustrated by Tony Morris

Legion of the White Tiger An exciting tale of high adventure, set in 38 B.C., describing the hazardous journey Cerdic and Festus make to 'the land beyond the North Wind'. Written by James Watson for older readers

Uncle Misha's Partisans Based on the lives of a group of real freedom fighters, this is the exciting story of a boy's determination to avenge his family killed by the Nazis in the Ukraine. By Yuri Suhl

New Beavers are published every month and if you would like the *Beaver Bulletin* – which gives all the details – please send a large stamped addressed envelope to:

Beaver Bulletin
The Hamlyn Group
Astronaut House
Feltham
Middlesex TW14 9AR